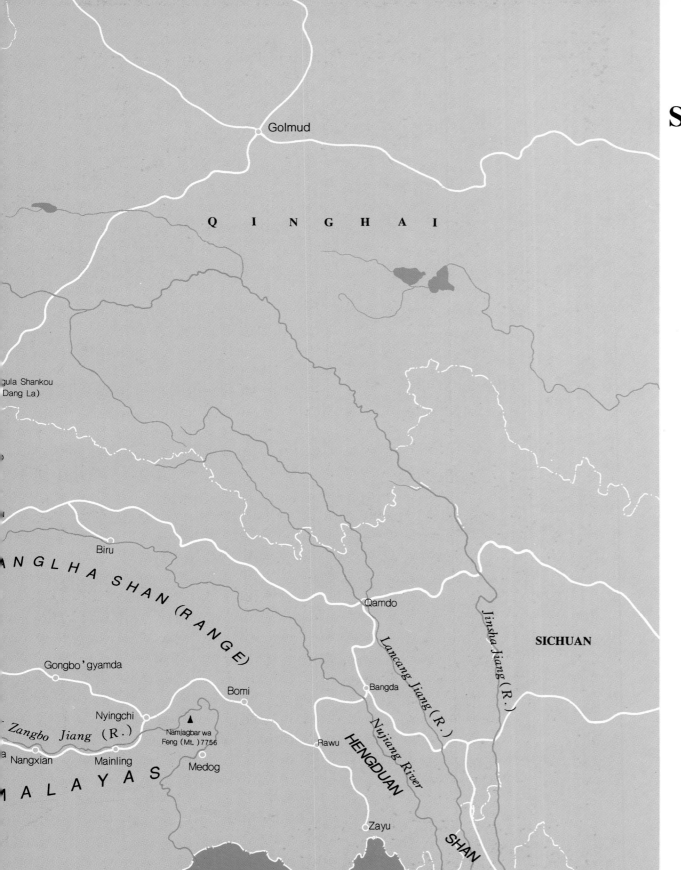

SKETCH TOUR MAP OF CHINA TIBET

Golmud

Q I N G H A I

gula Shankou
Dang La)

Biru

NGLHA SHAN (RANGE)

Gongbo'gyamda

Bomi

Nyingchi

Zangbo Jiang (R.)

Namjagbar wa
Feng (Mt.) 7756

Nangxian

Mainling

Medog

MALAYAS

Qamdo

Lancang Jiang (R.)

Jinsha Jiang (R.)

SICHUAN

Bangda

Rawu

HENGDUAN

Nujiang River

Zayu

SHAN

(MTS.)

YUNNAN

TRAVEL ON THE ROOF OF THE WORLD

——CHINA TIBET TOUR

Compiled by Tibet Tourism Bureau
and China Travel & Tourism Press

Published by China Travel & Tourism Press

（京）新登字 031 号

Advisor：Tang Zhengqi
Members of Comp ilatory Committee：Xiao Zhigang   Zhou Lizong
    Zhang Wansheng   Li Hongbu
    Gu Weiheng   Ma Jinkang   Zhou Jingcheng
    Bu Wangdui   Wang Xueyan
    Jin Mei   He Zhong
Editor－in－chief：Gu Weiheng
Vice Chief Editors：Jin Mei   Ma Jinkang   He Zhong   Bu Wangdui
Editors：Gu Weiheng   Xu Hua
Text by：Tang Zhengqi   Jin Mei   Ma Jinkang   Gu Weiheng   Li Zhirong
    He Zhong   Zhang Hui   Wang Hongmin   Wang Qiggelie
    Lan Bing   Chen Qing
Translated by：Liu Haiming   Chen Mingming   Ou Xiaomei   Liu Ling
Designer：Wen Heng   Hua Yi
Cartographer：Sun Suju
Photos by：Gu Weiheng   Zhang Ying   Du Zequan   Gu Shoukang
    Liu Wenmin   Yuan Xuejun   Liu Liqun   Yang Yichou
    Zhang Jiangyuan   Wen Heng   Ji Quan   Li Shuande   Yu Pengfei
    Jin Yaowen   Yuan Kezhong   Xu Zhenshi   Zhang Ying
    Gu Husheng   Bian Zhiwu   Chen Heyi   Li Changjie
    Li Bingyuan   YinLingbo   Ding Changzheng   Jin Mei
    Li Quunju   Le Jinxiong   Yu Yuntian   Li Jun   Sun Zhenhua
    Zong Tongchang   Meng Zi   Gong Weijian   He Zhong
    Ci Renduoji

图书在版编目（CIP）数据

在世界屋脊旅行:中国西藏旅游英文/西藏旅游局,中国旅
游出版社编著. —北京:中国旅游出版社,1994.12
ISBN 7－5032－1138－5

Ⅰ.在… Ⅱ.①西… ②中… Ⅲ.旅游－中国－西藏－英文
Ⅳ.F592.775
中国版本图书馆 CIP 数据核字(94)第 14471 号

Published by China Travel ＆ Tourism Press
Add：9A Jianguomennei Dajie, Beijing 100005, China
Tel：01－5138866－2024
Fax：01－5136282

CONTENTS

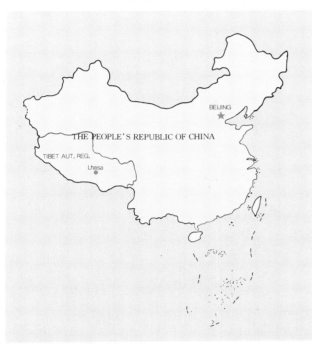

LOCATION OF TIBET IN MAP OF CHINA

Director of China Tibet Tourism Bureau
Tang Zhengqi

Preface

"Travel on the Roof of the World", an illustrated guide book compiled by the Tourism Bureau of Tibet Autonomous Region with support and assistance from the China Travel & Tourism Press, is finally ready for publication. To give the readers a better understanding of Tibet and travel in the region, the book is packed with lustrous pictures and information on tourism and aspects of life in Tibet. It is an indispensable guide to visitors to Tibet.

Tibet has long been known as the Roof of the World. It is in the southwestern part of China bordering India, Bhutan, Sikkim and Nepal. The region is full of spectacular skylines of majestic mountain peaks, breathtaking canyons, scattered highland lakes, rolling pasture and farm land, and pristine forests. The population of the region consists mostly of the Tibetans, Monbans and Lhobans, cultivating for centuries very unique ethnic traditions and glorious cultures unseen anywhere else. This is a land of enduring enchantment and tantalizing mystery. The resplendent scenes of nature and cultural traditions heavy with historical power are all resources for developing tourism in the region.

Spurred by China's policy of reform and opening to the outside world, Tibetan tourism began in 1980. So far the region has welcomed over 200,000 international visitors. A complete system of travel services of considerable scale has been under operation. The region now boasts of 26 tourist hotels with a combined capacity for 4,100 guests. Of the 10 hotels, three are of three-star standard, three two-stars and four one-stars. A total of 40 travel agencies are operating in the region, of which five are Class A agencies, six Class B and 29 Class C. Equipped with over 350 tourist vehicles, the three tourist car companies provide visitors with safe, quality and efficient services.

Over the past 14 years, tourism resources in the region have been continuously developed with Lhasa as the center and with tourist routes extending to Shigatse, Shannan, Nyingchi, Ngari and Nakchu, covering a total of over 60 scenic spots and places of interest. In addition to sightseeing tours, mountaineering, trecking and scientific tours are also available to meet needs of special interest visitors.

Tibet enjoys social stability and steady economic growth with people of divergent ethnic origins living peaceably together. As China's reform is moving further ahead, the infrastructure, communications and investment environment of Tibet are being steadily upgraded. Tibet, the roof of the world, is poised for 21st century and its warm-hearted and hospitable people welcome travellers, tourists and investors to the region.

Director of China Tibet Tourism Bureau

Welcome to "the Roof of the World"

— A Survey of Tourism in Tibet, China

The Qingzang Plateau, in the southwest of China, has long enjoyed a reputation of being "the Roof of the World", where Tibet Autonomous Region with an average altitude of over 4,000 meters and an area of 1.2 million square kilometers occupies a major portion. The majestic Tibetan highland stands on top of the world and its unique cultural tradition has an international fame. This is a land of vast contrast with snow-capped mountains offering beauty unsurpassed and deep tropical rain forests in another, and with open pasture land against imposing mountains and cornifer forests. The great Himalayas lies in its south with the towering Mt. Qomolangma standing above all world's peaks.

In addition to these spectacular offerings of Nature, the time-worn Tibetan cultural tradition is most enchanting. A glorious tradition mingled with wisdom of the Han and other ethnic peoples is represented by such achievements as the ancient Xiangxiong Culture ruins, Yumbu Lakang Palace, the ruins of ancient Guge Kingdom, the Potola Palace and Jokhang Temple. The population of the region consists mostly of the Tibetans, Monbans and Lhobans, all industrious and honest peoples full of wisdom and valor. Over the centuries, they have cultivated very unique ethnic traditions, folklores and ways of life, contributing to the Chinese civilization and human progress. This is a land of enduring enchantment and tantalizing mystery.

Since the early 1980s when Tibet began to open its long-closed doors to the outside world, tourism of the region has been growing with a continuous stream of mountaineers, explorers and tourists coming to the region. During the 14 years from 1980 through 1993, more than 200,000 visitors from over 60 countries and regions around the world visited Tibet for tourism, mountaineering and expeditions. The accommodation and transportation facilities for the tourism industry as well as the services have been greatly upgraded.

Tibet enjoys such unparalleled travel resources as Mt Qomolangma, the highest peak in the world on the Sino-Nepalese border, the winding Yarlung Zangbo River, ancient ruins, palaces and monasteries, folkloric activities and religious cer-

emonies. Tourism resources in the region have been continuously developed. Lhasa is now the tourist center with routes extending to Xigaze, Shannan, Nyingchi, Ngari and Nagqu, covering a total of over 60 scenic spots and places of interest.

Lhasa, "the Land of Gods" in Tibetan, sits on the north bank of River Lhasa, a tributary of the Yarlung Zangbo River, at an altitude of 3,700 meters. It has a history of over 13 centuries. With more than 3,000 hours of sunshine annually, Lhasa is famed as "the City of Sunshine" It is the capital of Tibet Autonomous Region and the center of Tibet's political, economic, cultural and religious activities. There are many historic sites and famous relics in the city proper and its suburbs, among which the Potola Palace, Jokhang Temple, Drepung Monastery, Sera Temple and Gandan Temple are world famous.

Shigatse (Xigaze), at an altitude of 3,800 meters, has a history of five centuries. A political and religious center for the Rear Tibet, it is also the town of traditional residence of Bainqen Lama. The majestic Himalayas are to the south of Shigatse. The Shrine of Amitabha Meitriya in the Tashilumpo Monastery has attracted throngs of visitors. Visitors to Shigatse can also visit the Sakya (Sagya) Monastery, Palcho Monastery and Shalu Monastery nearby.

Tsetang (Zetang), the birthplace of earliest Tibetans, sits on the south bank in the middle section of the Yarlung Zangbo River with a moderate climate at an altitude of 3,600 meters. The nearby Yalong River scenic area is a national scenic park with Samye Monastery, Yumbu Lakang Palace, burial site for Tsampos and Changzhu Monastery spotting the region.

Nyingchi is situated in the lower reach of the Yarlung Zangbo River with a mild and moist climate at an altitude of about 3,000 meters. The region has a concentration of Monba and Lhoba ethnic community with very unique customs. Mt Namjagbarwa, the great Himalayan Canyon, Lake Basumco and other unique scenery of natural wonder are also popular tourist attractions.

Ngari in the west of Tibet is famed as the top of "the Roof

of the World" with an average altitude of over 4,500 meters. It is sparsely populated and has some highland lakes, a haven for highland wildlife including yaks, antelopes and wild donkeys. The famous Guge ruins, Tuolin Monastery and Doxang are all in the western part of Ngari. The Sacred Mountain Kailash and Holy Lake Manasarova in Burang County are mecca to Chinese and foreign pilgrims.

Nakchu (Nagqu) area is also called the North Tibetan Plateau with an altitude of 4,500 meters. The Qingzang highway winds through the region providing easy passage amidst picturesque landscape. The ancient Zhangzhong culture ruins, Bonnist monastery, the holy Namco Lake and folklores of highland herders are all unique attractions to visitors from outside.

Chamdo is a region where the Hengduan Mountain Range, the Jinsha River, Nujiang River and Lanchang River converge. This rich and fertile valley has spectacular scenery, dense forests, ancient ruins and exotic ethnic groups, holding great fascination to visitors.

The tours in the region are mostly cultural and sightseeing in nature. However, special interest tours covering the full range of mountaineering, trekking, sceintific exploration, folklore studies and religious pilgrimage are also on the rise.

Cultural and Sightseeing Tours Many visitors travelling to Tibet hope to experience the ancient cultural and religious traditions of Tibet, its breathtaking highland scenery and exotic folklores and customs. For this purpose, Lhasa, Shigatse and Shannan are ideal destinations.

Trekking Tourists can travel on foot along country footpaths, traditional vendors' trails and pilgrimage routes to select destinations, with equipment and supplies carried by animals and porters. Mt Qomolangma and Mt Shishabangma (Xixabangma) as well as the Holy Mountain and Sacred Lake in Ngari are the most popular areas for trekking.

Special Tours The following routes are offered for special tours: Lhasa — the base camp of Mt Qomolangma; Lhasa — Xigaze — Ngari; Gandan Monastery — Samye Monastery; Gyamagou — Qingpu — Samye.

Scientific Expedition Tours Tibet has also been

known as "the Third Pole" of the earth. The Himalaya Range, and the topography, climate, rivers, lakes, glaciers, permafrost regions, the fauna and flora of Tibet have attracted many scientists and explorers from both China and overseas.

Mountaineering Tour   Tibet possesses exceptional charms unfound anywhere else for mountaineers. The 2,000-km stretch along southern Tibet, which forms the northern slopes of the Himalayas, has five peaks more than 8,000 meters above the sea level, plus over 70 peaks between the range from 7,000 to 8,000 meters and over 3,000 peaks higher than 6,000 meters. The region from Mount Qomolangma to Mount Shishabangma are the most challenging to professional mountaineers from around the world.

Religious Tours   Tibet has been famed for its many temples and monasteries. The Tibetan Buddhism as the important part of Tibetan traditional culture has persisted for over ten centuries. Wherever you go in Tibet, be it a mountain pass, or a desolate lakeside or mountain village, you are bound to see colorful sutra streamers hung here and there and offerings made for religious purpose. A familiar sight is monks in dark red praying each step of their way. The air is charged with religious piety and mystery. Its various sacred buildings with very unique designs and outlines are always enchanting to travellers.

Folklore Study Tours   The Tibetans and other ethnic minorities of the region have cultivated living traditions over the centuries as practiced in festival celebrations, marriage and funeral rituals, farming and ways of life. Their costumes, music and dance are also truly colorful and full of dynamism to visitors.

Transportation   Tibet is the only region in China with no railways. Currently, the main means of travel into the area are by air and land vehicles.

Airlines   Tibet has opened international and inter-provincial air routes. The flights from Lhasa to Chengdu, Beijing, Chongqing and Kathmandu of Nepal provide quick entry and exit for travellers to the region. The Gonggar Airport is located 100 km south of Lhasa, just one and a half hours' drive.

Large passenger planes including Boeing 747 can land on the airport. The modern airport terminal can hold 600 people at peak time. The Bangda Airport at Chamdo(Qamdo), claimed to be of the highest elevation among modern airports in the world, has successfully passed a trial run and can handle the landing of Boeing 757

Highways   The main highways leading into Tibet include the 736-km-long Sino-Nepalese Highway between Lhasa and the Friendship Bridge Pass at Zhangmu; the Qinghai-Tibetan Highway, a 1,214-km-long asphalt road linking Golmud and Lhasa with an average elevation of over 4,000 meters, main road passing through the Kunlun and Tanggula Mountains and the Nyainqêntanglha Range.

The road network in Tibet Autonormous Region consists of 15 main roads and 315 secondary roads with a total length of 22,000 km open to traffic. A road network has been initially formed with its hub around Lhasa and with the Chengdu-Lhasa, Golmud-Lhasa, Xinjiang-Tibet, Yunnan-Tibet and China-Nepal highways as mainstays. Arterial highways include the Lhasa-Yadong, Heihe-Ngari, Shigatse-Burang, Heihe-Qamdo, Nyingchi-Tsetang, Lhasa-Tsetang, Tsetang-Cona, Lhasa-Shigatse and Lhasa-Zhangmu highways.

Currently, the tourist agencies in Tibet have 350 foreign made mini-buses and land rovers of different kinds with a total of over 4,000 seats and an annual transporting capacity of 50,000 passengers.

Hotels   The number of tourst hotels in the region has increased over the past few years to a total of 26.

Travel Agencies   A total of 36 travel agencies are operating in the region, of which five are Class A agencies capable of organizing tours directly for international visitors, six Class B for operating tours in the regioin.

Food   Hotels in Tibet offer delicious food which is predominantly Sichuan cuisine. The Holiday Inn Lhasa offers a European fare for the international visitors while the Tsetang Hotel in Shannan is known for its authentic Cantonese cooking. Buffets are popular and Tibetan food is available for those who wish to try the exotic. A number of fine restaurants have the

official license of the tourism administration in Lhasa, Shigatse and Tsetang.

Shopping   Tibetan rugs, coasters, traditional aprons, costumes, hats and boots, and jewlery and a dazzling array of handcraft articles are all made by hand with meticulous craftsmanship and intricate designs true to the age-old tradition. These articles are available at gift shops at different hotels and street markets at Barkor Street in old town of Lhasa, in Shigatse and Tsetang.

Entertainment   Tibet is often described by travellers as "a place of festive of song and dance" The folk songs and dances of the region are spectacularly colorful and promise exotic enchantment.

Traditional Festivals   Tibet has many many festivals of ethnic and religious nature throughout the year, which include the Tibetan New Year, the Shoton Festival, the Bathing Festival, the Butter Lantern Festival and the Horse-race Festival, celebrating a tradition that has been cultivated for centuries.

Tibet, loftly located on "the Roof of the World", offers a special appeal and enchantment to travellers, scholars, explorers and even those with an artistic bend its majestic landscape, colorful folk tradition and a time-worn cultural heritage. Many travellers have longed to adventure into this land of ultimate mystery.

This illustrated guide book attempts to answer the questions any prospective traveller to the region may have regarding how to go about travelling in Tibet, what to see on different tour routes, how to arrange accommodation, transport and food, and where to obtain information and assistance. We hope the book will prove both a valuable companion and a momento for a journey that is bound to leave indelible impression.

Welcome to Tibet !

12

I. Lhasa, the Sacred Land

Lhasa, likely to be the most exotic and enchanting city in the world, often offers its newly arrived visitors a dizzying welcome because of its elevation of 3,700 meters above the sea level. A history of 13 centuries has enriched the city with a wealth of cultural heritage and an ever-present religious piety. A visit to Lhasa is a tour into history. In an era when city skylines crowd our visual landscapes, Lhasa offers a pleasant and soothing retreat and seclusion with its primeval simplicity and pastoral serenity.

Before the mid-seventh century when Lhasa, later a central town of Tibetan region, was yet to come into being, the area called Wotang was a marshy land of wildness, frequented by antelopes. On one bright summer day, Songtsan Gampo, leader of the Tubo tribe that had risen to power in the Yarlong River Valley, was struck by the perilous position of an area flanked by two steep mountains, while bathing in the Lhasa River, and decided that this was to be the home of his kingdom. This ambitious Tibetan king moved the center of his rule to Wotang and ordered the construction of his residence on the hilltop of Potala. In A.D. 641, Songtsan Gampo who by this time had conquered the whole Tibetan region wedded Princess Wencheng of the Imperial Tang Court. When the princess arrived, she became convinced that Lake Wotang was a devil's heart to be overpowered by the construction of a grand temple after filling up the lake with earth. The princess further suggested that the earth be carried by white goats. This imposing grand temple became a symbol of the kingdom. The temple, later known as Jokhang, was initially named Lhasa, "The Sacred Land" in Tibetan. Over the centuries, Lhasa became a political and religious center of Tibet. Administrative orders were issued from the myriad of imposing palaces; the great temples and monasteries were home to omnipotent liturgical establishment and witnessed the rise of many religious leaders and endless religous ceremonies. The faithful composed the population of the town and Lhasa became a true "Mecca" of Tibet.

The visitors to Tibet never fail to notice the generous sunshine, estimated to be more than 3,000 hours annually. Glittering pinnacles of temples and monasteries against the vault of big skies, and bright buildings and cheerful crowds hemmed in by steep mountains, are a permanent image of Lhasa. In this city of sunshine, an ever-present historical and religious solemnity is highlighted by the bright sunshine. The Potala Palace is a symbol of majestic nobleness while Norbu Lingka is pure gracefulness. Drepung and Sera monasteries are evidence of the glory and extravagance of Tibetan Buddhism. The throngs of pilgrims crowd the steps of Jokhang Monastery. This is also a town of sharp contrasts: in the streets and alleyways, you may see modern shops and trendy youth mingled with pious pilgrims praying each step of their way; motor vehicles competing for passage with leisurely cattle and sheep. The Barkor Street circling the Jokhang Monastery is the center of the old town, much as it was centuries ago, where you may get a feel of local life and bargain for handcraft articles. This holy town of many gods is such a mixture of past and present, the secular and sacred, clamor and serenity, reminiscence and abandonment, all contributing to the city's mystery, cheerfulness and enduring charm.

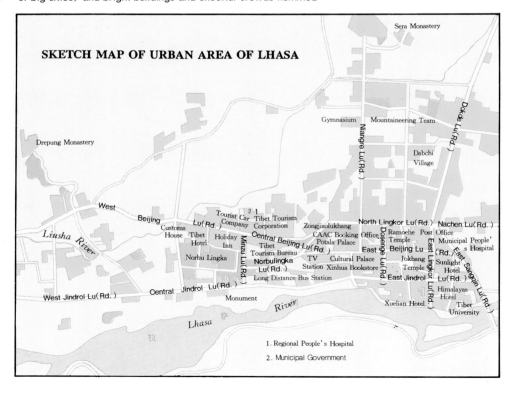

SKETCH MAP OF URBAN AREA OF LHASA

1. Regional People's Hospital
2. Municipal Government

◁ Morning of Potala Palace

Gilded Tops (Roofs) of Potala Palace

Pillars in White Palace of Potala

White Palace of Potala Palace

▷ Potala Palace in Summer

Bedroom in White Palace of Potala

Mural：Extending Potala Palace

Drawing Room in White Palace of Potala

Mural：The Fifth Dalai Lama Received in Audience by Qing Emperor Shunzhi

Statue of Songtsan Gampo

Peacock

Statue of Princess Wencheng

Lions

Door knocker

Painted wood carving on the structure

◁ Holy Bird and Dragon King's Daughter
（Wood carving）

Gold diploma and seal granted to the 13th
Dalai Lama by Qing Government

Bronze Statue o Tsong Khapa in Potala Palace

Pearly Mandala in Stupa-tomb of 13th Dalai

Main Statue of Buddha shrined in Potala Palace

Religious wine vessel made of numan skull

Mandala （altar） in Potala Palace

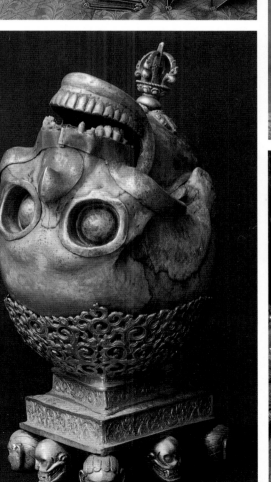

New Palace in Norbu Lingka   Top of Gate to Norbu Lingka

Throne in New Palace

Chair-bed in the New Palace

Tibetan-style door in Norbu Lingka

Scene before Jokhang Temple at
festival

Gilded roofs of the Jokhang Temple

Gilded scripture streamers

Scripture wheels in Jokhang Temple

Scripture-chanting lamas

Statue of Sakyamuni brought to Jokhang
Temple by Princess Wencheng

Interior view of Jokhang Temple

Butter lamps in Jokhang Temple

Worshipping outside Jokhang Temple

◁ Devout Buddhists

Barkhor Street

With best wishes

Bronze statue of Buddha's Warrior
Attendant Shengle in Drepung Monastery

Big Scripture Hall in Drepung Monastery

Masks in Sera Monastery

Scripture-debating in Sera Monastery

Mt. Yaowangshan

Tangka（scroll paintings）of traditional
Tibetan medicine

Scripture streamers on the bridge of
Taiyang Dao（Sun Islet）

Lamas of Ramoche Monastery making
Tibetan medicine

◁ Tsongjiaolukang

Holy stupa for Tsong Khapa in Gandan Monastery

Scripture Hall，Gandan Monastery

Tibetan carpets

Monument Commemorating the

Sichuan-Tibet and Qinghai-Tibet

Highways Opening to Traffic

Mane Pile

Yak-hide boat on the Yarlung Zangbo River

II. Tour in Southeast Tibet
— Pearls of the Plateau: Shannan, Nyingchi and Chamdo

The southeastern Tibet is a majestic and mysterious highland area where the great mountain ranges of Himalaya, Nyanchen Tanglha and Hengduan converge. The unusual terrain has created the most spectacular scenery, unique local climate and dense forests. The towering snow-capped mountain peaks, glaciers, river rapids, waterfalls, cloud shrouded ancient monasteries, holy mountains and lakes are common sights in this region of mystery and enchantment.

The southeastern Tibet is not only known for its spectacular landscape. It also has an ancient history and esoteric religious tradition which have made local culture all the more fascinating and awe-inspiring.

The area is inhabited by the Tibetan, Lhoban, Monban, Naxi and Den people whose primitive life style and warm-hearted hospitality are always refreshing and exhilarating to visitors. Shannan, Nyingchi and Chamdo (Qamdo) are the three jewels of this land of riches.

The road from Lhasa crosses the Yarlung Zhangbo River and, after extending some distance, leads into Shannan area.

This area is rich and fertile which witnessed the emergence of the Tibetan people and the rise of the Tubo Kingdom. The Ya long River Scenic Area is designated as the only national scenic area in Tibet. It includes Yumbu Lakang, the earliest palace in Tibet, the burial ground for the kings of the Tubo kingdom between the seventh and ninth centuries and the Changzhu Temple, the earliest temple of Buddhism in Tibet, built in the seventh century. The Samye Monastery, the earliest of its kind in Tibet, sits on the northern bank of the Yarlung Zhangbo River. The legendary monkey cave is half way up the Kongbo Mountain, just behind the Zedang(Tsetang) town seat in Shannan. The picturesque Yamzhog Yumco Lake, Gyaca Lake and Zegu pasture land are popular scenic areas.

Nyingchi(Nyingtri) is known for its mild climate and lush vegetation. Go eastward from Lhasa and, after climbing the 4,700-meter-high Mila Mountain , you will come into an area with more and more trees and growing humidity. Cogao Lake, Niangpugou, Bayi Town and Bajila Scenic areas, Bujiu Monastery, Nanyi Valley, Lhoba Village and the ancient burial ground of Lieshan dot this region of dense forest. The Yarlung Zhangbo River cuts through the Himalayas, forming the Grand Yarlung Zhangbo Canyon, the deepest in the world, at the foot of Mt. Namjagbawa. The Medog Nature Reserve is famed for its great variety of rare species of plants. The Zayu area with semi-tropical climate and vegetation is popular with nature-loving travellers.

Chamdo is a region where the Hengduan Mountain Range, the Jinsha River, Nujiang River and Lanchang River converge. This rich and fertile valley has spectacular scenery, dense forests, ancient ruins and exotic ethnic groups. The Qiangbalin Monastery and Kanuo Ruins hold great fascination to visitors with their historical and religious mystery.

The newly opened Lhasa-Nyingchi- Tse tiang-Lhasa tour route will take you to the two enchanting jewels of the region. With the completion of the modern Bangda Airport in Chamdo, the town will be within easy access to Lhasa.

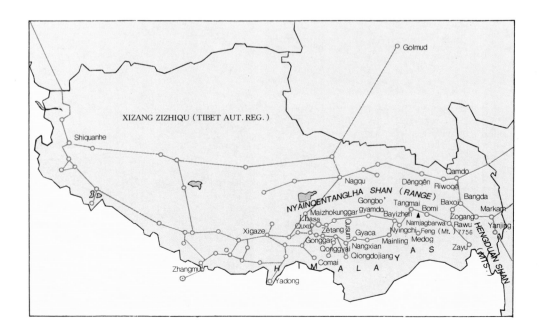

◁ Morning at the Yarlung Zangbo River

Drum beaters of Samye Monastery

Murals in Samye Monastery

Farm field in Shannan Prefecture

Hall of Samye Monastery

Tomb of Tibetan King in 7th century

Zuowu Dance of Shannan Prefecture

Yumbu Lakang—the First Palace in Tibet

Stone tablet to the Tomb of Tibetan King

Pearly tangka in Chamzhu Temple

Shannan Woman

Gyastsa Gorge on Yarlung Zangbo River

Evening glow over Mt. Namjagbawa

Scenery of Nyingchi

Zhasongcuo Lake

Tea Plantation at Yigong

Autumn scene of Doxiongna

Big Bend of Yarlung Zangbo River

A child of Gongbo

A Lhoba hunter

Gliding cable — means for crossing river

Monban women in Medog harvesting upland rice

Lamalin Monastery

Rainbow over an ancient fort

Tibetan-style wooden bridge

Autumn at Bowo

Rattan network bridge at Medog

Spring at Zayu

Tibetan girls in Zayu

Sichuan-Tibet Highway

Rawu Lake

Women in Rioche，Chamdo

Shepherd girl

Stone statue of Buddha in Jambalin
Lamasery

Dagobas beside a village

Iron-bar Lama（for enforcing force）in Jambalin Monastery

White-lip deer

A Tibetan crow

A tree frog (Rhacophorus leucomystax)

Ailurus fulgens (Lesser panda)

Zingiber Officinale

Puma

Gymnocypris przewalskii (Scaleless carp)
in the Yarlung Zangbo River

III. Charming Northern Tibet Plateau

The northern highland in Tibet is a vast region about 2,400 km in length and 700 km in width flanked by the great Kunlun and Tanggula mountain ranges on the one side and the Gangdisê, Nyenchen Tanglha mountain ranges on the other. The region with an average elevation of over 4,500 meters above sea level covers about two thirds of Tibet. The frost period lasts nine months here. The topography of the region is one of rolling hills with basins and highland lakes. Steaming hot springs can also be seen in the region.

In the animist tradition, the Tibetans believe that there is a god embodied in every mountain and lake. The region is therefore full of mountains and lakes deemed holy with mythic powers by the local people. Namco Lake with a surface area of 1,940 square km(about 70 km long and 30 km wide) and elevation of 4,718 meters is revered as a holy or celestial lake. The breath-taking scenery and many myths about the lake have attracted an endless stream of travellers and pilgrims. The vast and fertile pasture land around the lake is grazing ground for cattle all the year round. It is also frequent-ed by wild yaks and blue sheep.

There is a vast "uninhabited land" bordering Ngari and Nagqu(Nakchu), an area of 200,000 square km with an aver-age elevation of 5,000 meters above sea level. This region of extremities is a haven for wildlife. The travellers to the region often find company in packs of galloping wild donkeys, an-telopes and wild yaks.

The northern Tibet plateau is not only known for its spec-tacular scenery but is also a major pasture region with a rich variety of flora (over a hundred species) and mineral re-sources. The Tibetan yaks and blue sheep dot the pasture land. The town of Nagqu(Nakchu) by the Qinghai-Tibetan Highway is a political, business, cultural center of northern Ti-bet accessible by a network of roads. The annual Horse-race Festival held at the town is a window of highland culture and folklore activities. Nagqu and Damxung Horse Race festivals are the most lavishly celebrated festivals in northern Tibet.

The festival, held in August, the best time of the year, is attended by tens of thousands of herders coming on horseback from as far as hundreds of kilometers away. A white tent city emerges from nowhere. Contests of archery on horseback and horsemanship and yak race will be held at the festival together with performances by itinerant balladers and dancers in addi-tion to a lively swap market. A travellers' resort village has been completed outside Nagqu. Open all the year round, it of-fers interesting insight into local life style and folk activities to tourists.

The enchanting northern highland of Tibet, with breath-taking scenery and exhilarating warmth and simplicity of the local pastoral life, will give its visitors the experience of a lifetime.

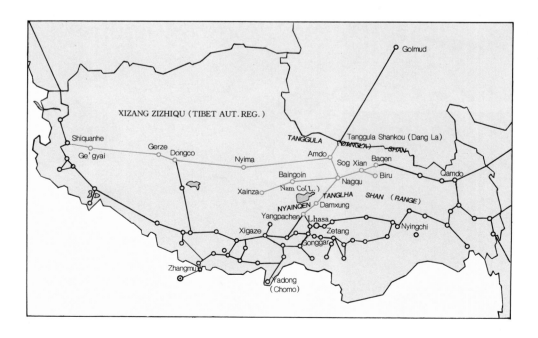

◁ Crane shot of Lake Namtso

Beautiful Northern Tibet Plateau

Grassland on Plateau

Lakeside of Namtso

Water of Holy Lake

Rainbow over the Plateau

Antelopes in the depopulated zone of
Northern Tibet

Wild donkeys in Northern Tibet

Wild yaks

Nakchu in August

Horse-racing

Audience

Lama musicians

Before the contest begins

Having a rest

Milking a yak

A folk artist performing the ballad "King Gesar"

Enthusiastic audience

Shearing

Pretty plaits

Churning woman

Xiaodeng Monastery

A tourist village at Nakchu

Weaving coloured belt

Luxurious ornaments

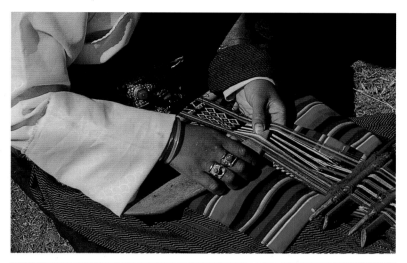

Temperature of Four Cities（Towns）of Tibet Autonomous Region

Month	Lhasa		Xigaze		Zetang		Nyingchi	
	Highest	Lowest	Highest	Lowest	Highest	Lowest	Highest	Lowest
January	6.8	−10.2	5.7	−13.1	7.6	−9.0	7.9	−5.3
February	9.2	−6.9	8.0	−9.5	9.9	−5.9	9.8	−2.7
March	12.0	−3.2	11.0	−5.4	12.9	−2.4	13.0	−0.1
April	15.7	0.9	15.5	−0.7	16.9	1.3	16.5	3.2
May	19.7	5.1	19.5	3.4	20.4	5.2	18.8	6.80
June	22.5	9.2	22.1	7.6	22.9	8.9	20.9	10.0
July	21.7	9.9	21.0	8.7	22.5	10.1	22.1	11.2
August	20.7	9.4	19.6	8.1	21.5	9.5	22.1	10.7
September	19.6	7.6	18.7	5.8	20.5	7.6	20.3	9.2
October	16.4	1.4	15.2	−1.2	17.1	1.8	17.2	4.9
November	11.6	−5.0	10.7	−8.0	12.4	−4.1	12.9	−0.7
December	7.7	−9.1	7.0	−12.3	8.7	−7.9	9.6	−4.5
Average Temperature	15.3	0.8	14.5	−1.4	15.5	1.3	15.9	3.6

Altitude of Lakes on Tour Routes in Tibet

Lake Name	Location	Altitude（m）	
Nam Co	Baingoin, Damxung	4718	Salty, 35 m deep
Manasarova	Burang	4588	Fresh, 81 m deep
Yamzho Yumco	Nagarze	4441	Salty, 51 m deep
Langa Co	Burang	4561	
Paiku Co	Gyirong	4591	Salty
Lake Cuogao	Gongbo gyamda	3460	Barrier Lake
Bangong Co	Rutog	4241	Fresh in east, salty in west 41.3m deep
Rawu	Baxoi	3850	
Zhari Nam Co	Coqen	4613	Salty
Dajia Co	Saga	5170	
Siling Co	Nyima	4530	Salty
Tangra Yumco	Nyima	4535	Salty

IV. Richly Endowed Gyangtse

Crossing the Yarlung Zhangbo River Bridge south of Lhasa and moving on southward, one comes to the Kampala Pass over 5,000 meters above sea level. Looking further south from this imposing pass, he will see a placid lake extending to the horizon. That is Yamzhog Yumco Lake, one of the three greatest holy lakes in Tibet, with a surface area of 638 square km and elevation of 4,441 meters. The lake has over 20 islets on it and rich and picturesque pasture ground rings the lake. Driving further west from the lake, one will enter the fertile Gyangze (Gyangtse) valley along the Nyangchu River after passing a chain of snow-capped mountain peaks with the highest being Mt. Nojin Gangsang. The region is known as a granary of Tibet.

The ancient town of Gyangze has a history of over six centuries. It sits by the road from Lhasa to Sagya, Xigaze and Yadong and has from ancient times been a center where pilgrims, merchants and travellers converge.

The Palcho Monastery in Gyangze was founded at a time when rivalry among Buddhist denominations reached an impasse. Hence it has been home to a number of Buddhist sects practicing under one roof with each occupying six to seven halls. The construction of the monastery began in the beginning of the 15th century. The three-story main hall houses an enormous bronze statue of the Buddha, about eight meters in height with a great number of tangkas on display. In both east and west wings at the second floor of the main hall are clay arhats from the Ming Dynasty. These true to life images are really a marvel and venerated throughout Tibet. The 32-meter-high white Palcho Pagoda has a total of 77 rooms with 108 doors at its nine levels. It houses a great number of miniature Buddha paintings, estimated at about 100,000 altogether, and is other wise known as "The Pagoda of 100,000 Buddha Images". This imposing octagonal structure is the most awe-inspiring of all pagodas in Tibet. The Palcho Pagoda's liturgical collection also includes a total of over 1,000 clay, bronze and gilded sculptures of the Buddha in addition to a great number of tangkas. The religious art and the Palcho architecture are renowned for their unique style.

The town of Gyangze is also known for its patriotic tradition. It withstood a brutal British invasion in 1904. The fortresses on Zhongshanbao built in defence against British troops remain as witness to the past heroic battles.

The handcraft art of Gyangze is popular with visitors. The Tibetan rugs, coasters and daggers are uniquely crafted and much sought after by tourists.

Gyangze is accessible by road from different directions. It has roads leading to Lhasa and Shannan to the east, Xigaze to the north, Tingri through Kampa and Dinggyê to the west, and the border station of Yadong through picturesque Yadong valley in the Himalaya mountains to the south.

Visitors are drawn to the ancient town of Gyangze by its rich cultural tradition, exotic architecture, epic history and unique handcraft art. More tour routes will be opened for this region of plenty and beauty.

Wanfo (Ten-Thousand-Buddha) Pagoda at Palcho Lamasery

Bird's-eye view of Lake Yamdotso

Dawn at Zhongshan

Courtyard of ordinary Tibetan residence

Gate of local residence

Coloured painting on the pagoda in Palcho Temple

Rape flower

Two yaks harnessed on a bar ploughing

Sculpturer of Tingri

Making carpets

Head-dress of Kangmar woman

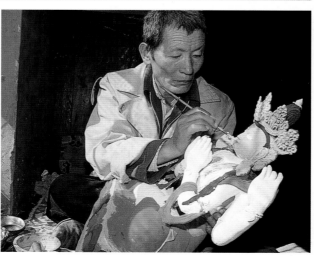

◁ **Wall of ancient Sheger County Government Seat**

Scenery of Pagri

Scenery of Yadong

Ruins of Gangba County Government Seat

Ancient object of worship in Tinggye

V. Shigatse — Center of Rear Tibet

The town of Shigatse(Xigaze) sits at the confluence of Nyangchu and Yarlung Zhangbo rivers about 250 km to the west of Lhasa. This second largest city in Tibet at an elevation of 3,800 meters has a history of more than five centuries. The region around is historically known as the Rear Tibet and Xigaze has been its political, business, cultural and religious center. The residence for all the Bainqen Lamas has been traditionally in the town.

The Tashilhunpo Monastery in the west can be seen in the distance by travellers approaching the town, with its gilded pinnacle glinting in the sunshine, an exhilarating sight to arriving wayfarers and pilgrims. The construction of Tashilhunpo (meaning "imminent bless") began in 1447. The Monastery is the largest of its kind in Rear Tibet with a total floor space of 300,000 square meters. The Great Prayer Hall, the oldest building in the monastery, can house over 2,000 praying monks. The lavish throne of Bainqen, a myriad of Buddhist sculptures and ancient murals are rare treasures of the monastery. Jamkhang, the chapel of Maitreya with a height of 30 meters and a total of seven stories, is the central structure of the monastery. Enshrined inside the chapel is a giant 26.5-meter-high sculpture of Maitreya with its middle fingers measured 1.2 meters and the shoulder 11.5 meters. A total of 115,875 kilograms of copper and 6,700 ounces of gold in addition to a great number of diamonds, pearls and amber pieces were used for the construction of the image, which is a fine example of the Tibetan artistry and craftsmanship.

The funerary stupas in the monastery are also worth noting with the most lavishly furnished being that for Bainqen IV (1567-1662). The construction of the hall housing the stupa took four years to complete. The stupa is 11 meters high. It was built with over 2,700 ounces of gold, 33,000 ounces of silver and 39,000 kilograms of copper and is adorned with about 9,000 feet of silk and over 7,000 pearls, gems and agate, coral pieces. The religious ornaments on the gilded pinnacle of the stupa building are of interesting designs and exquisite artistry.

East of Tashilhunpo is a huge structure constructed with stone blocks against a hill slope of nearly 100 meters in height. Every year, a ceremony is held to air an enormous tapestry of the image of the Buddha hung on the stone surface. There is also an unusual room in this monastery unseen in others for the display of portraits of Qing Dynasty emperors and gifts to Bainqen from the imperial court. It was also once used by Bainqen to meet envoys from the court and receive imperial decrees. A collection of rare treasures and artifacts are stored in this room.

Built in 1087, the Shalu Monastery in Shigatse is known for its unique architecture integrating both Han and Tibetan styles unparalleled anywhere else in Tibet. It houses a rich collection of ancient frescos strongly influenced by Song and Yuan Dynasty art. The collection is in very good condition.

Xigaze region enjoys a moderate climate with plenty of sunshine. The fertile river valley is one of the granaries of Tibet. The town proper has undergone a construction boom with roads leading to Ngari in the west, the Qomolangma Nature Reserve and border with Nepal in the south, Nagqu to the north and Lhasa and Shannan to the east.

The ancient town of Xigaze has become well-known for its past and rich cultural tradition with Palcho, Sagya, Pingcuolin and Juenang monasteries and Pala Estate as well as the Qomolangma Nature Reserve covering an area of over 30,000 square kilometers in the nearby region. The annual ceremony of display of Buddha tapestry, the Sorcerer's Dance Festival, the Ximuqingpo Festival at Shalu Monastery and the active local Tibetan theater are popular attractions to visitors.

With its rich cultural tradition, majestic monasteries, breath-taking scenery and convenient location, Shigatse (Xigaze) has become one of the most popular tourist destinations in Tibet.

Statue of Amitabha Meitriya — 26.5 m tall, the biggest indoor gilded copper Buddha in the world

Tashilhunpo Temple at dawn   Gilded silver sacrificial lamps   Part of gilded roof top of Tashilhunpo Temple

Scripture debating lamas in Tashilhunpo
Monastery

Stupa for the 4th Panchen in Tashilhunpo
Temple

Butter offerings

Bronze statue of Buddha's Warrior
Attendant

A lama carrying water

New Palace of Panchen

Seat-bed in the New Palace of Panchen

Song and dance "Jiexie" of Rear Tibet

Gaben（Chief）musician

Playing classic music "Gaer"

A praying old woman

Evil-dispelling designs on door of local
residential house in Shigatse

Masked donkey

A trivial sight

Fetching water from Yarlung Zangbo
River

Juelang Monastery in Lhatsê

Shalu Monastery

VI. Sakya Monastery
— A Treasure House of Tibetan Arts and Culture

In A.D. 1073, Gongjue Jiebu of the Kun family in Tibet built a monastery on a meadow shaped like a lying elephant on the north bank of Zongqu River to teach his new esoteric theory of Buddhism. Gongjue Jiebu was convinced that the monastery built on such a site would light the mundane world. Because the monastery was built by a chalky hill, it was named Sakya, meaning chalky earth in Tibetan. However, few expected that it would later become the name of a powerful Buddhist denomination and ruling house owing to a number of political and religious factors. The Sakya Monastery built by Gongjue Jiebu (popular known as the North Temple) became inadequate for rising and evermore powerful Sakya establish - ment. A larger monastery which is still standing today was built on the south bank of Zongqu River by the Kun house and Pagpa, a well-known Tibetan in the Mongolian imperial court of the 13th century. This monastery, now popularly known as the South Sakya, sits against the backdrop of snow-capped mountains 165 km west of Xigaze.

In A. D. 1260, Pagpa was appointed the imperial tutor and later an official in charge of Buddhist affairs in the land and ruler of whole of Tibet by Kublai Khan, the first emperor of the Yuan Dynasty. In 1267, Pagpa returned to Tibet to establish the Sakya Kingdom and a Tibetan government subordinate to Yuan Dynasty rule. A mural in the monastery depicts the occasion when Pagpa as the supreme ruler of the region gave the commission to Segasan Bu in 1288 for the construction of the monastery, which involved labor and material contributions from 130,000 Tibetan households. The Sakya Monastery as the power center of the Sakya Kingdom once ruled the whole Tibet for more than a century.

When the visitor approaches this massive structure, he will see a great monastery in an imposing square citadel. The outer wall is painted red, white and black, each representing the different manifestations of Buddha, a unique feature of Sakya. The Lakang Qinmu Hall, the main structure in the complex, occupies an area of 5,500 square meters with a height of over 10 meters. According to monastery records, the hall had 108 giant columns. Now there are only 40 left, with many anecdotes about them. The monastery wall is 10 meters high and over three meters thick. The northern and southern walls are 500 meters in length while the eastern and western walls 300 meters. There are a total of 40 fortresses and four pillboxes along the entire length of the wall and four gates open in different directions. The remnants of a moat is still visible. The entire complex gives a feeling of solemnity laden with the weight of history.

The Sakya Monastery is also known for its collection of Tangkas and scriptures. The monastery also has a great collection of appointment letters, official seals, head decorations and costumes granted to Sakya officials by the imperial court of Yuan Dynasty, in addition to Buddhist figurines, ceremonial artifacts and porcelain ware from the Song and Yuan dynasties onward. The stupendous collection of books cover religion, history, medicine, philosophy, calendar, theatre, poetry, stories and grammar and are valuable source materials for the study of ancient Tibetan culture. The Sakya collection of Buddhist scriptures is also the largest in Tibet with a total of 40,000 volumes, of which over 10,000 are kept in the main hall. They were meticulously hand written in red and black ink with many gold and silver letterings by calligraphers called in from all Tibet by Pagpa. The scripture written on "Pattra" leaves recently discovered is regarded as a rare treasure.

The murals and tangkas in the monastery are unique, of which a large mural of the five Sakya founders and an exquisite mural of mandalas are of particular interest. A total of 40 tangkas depicting the founders of Sakya painted six centures ago is a treasure to the monastery. When the visitor stands in front of the pictures of these noted figures in Tibetan history, he is bound to feel the power of the glory of a bygone era and of an art that shines through the darkness of time. Sakya can be compared to Dunhuang in western China. In fact, it is regarded as second Dunhuang of China.

Gate

Grand Scripture Hall in Sakya Lamasery

Gold Statue of Buddha

Pillars of Scripture Hall

Mural walls of Mandalas（enclosed altar town）

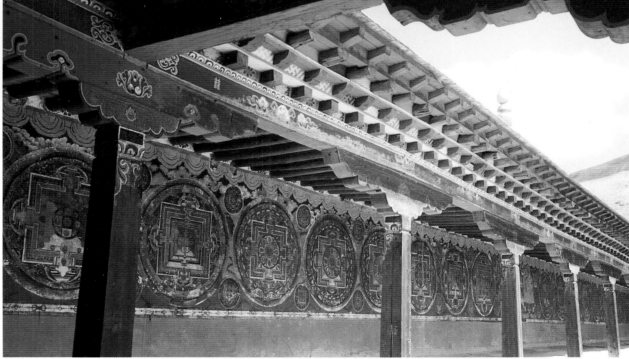

Throne for Buddhist King in Sakya
Monastery

Chair for Abbot in Scripture Hall

Thick wall of the Lamasery

Ruins of Northern Sakya Lamasery

Scene of Sakya County Seat

Mural: Kublai Khan receiving Pagpa

Conch — a precious holy object   Gold seal fo Bailan King   Porcelain lion made in Yuan Dynasty

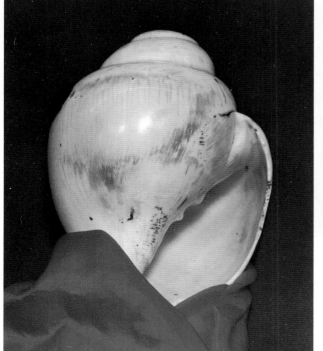

Murals made in Yuan Dynasty

Scriptures written in gold ink on bookshelf

Pattra-leaf scripture

Micro masks

Scripture written in gold ink in Yuan Dynasty

Tangka（Tibetan scroll painting）:
The Black Wrathful Devi

▷ Tangka（Tibetan scroll painting）: Lion- head

Goddess（Sangdongma）

▷ Tangka （Tibetan scroll painting）:
Bangongxia

Tangka （Tibetan scroll painting）: Buzha

▷ Old woman of Sakya in local costume
Deep in thought

VII. Majestic Mount Qomolangma (Everest)
— The Beautiful Third Goddess

Over one and a half centuries ago, when European travellers first had a glimpse of Mt Qomolangma from a distance of 240 km in the northern Indian plain, they had no idea that this imposing mountain on the Sino-Nepalese border was the highest mountain on earth. Not until 1852 did people realize that the mountain seen by the Europeans in 1849 dwarfs all others. As more and more people became fascinated by the spectacular views of Mt. Qomolangma and aware of its sacredness in the heart of peoples inhabitating the area around it and the many myths about it, the mountain together with its many sister peaks (four above 8000 meters and 38 above 7000 meters) came to be known as the "third pole of the earth."

Mt Qomolangma with an altitude of 8,846.27 meters is located in the southern part of Tingri County of Tibet in the middle section of the Himalayas. Its perpetually snow-capped peak is truly spectacular with many glaciers and sharp ice precipices. Below the snowline, ice blocks line, winding glaciers and treacherous ice holes present scenes of sheer beauty.

The rise of Mt Qomolangma began only two million years ago, much later than the advent of mankind. However, its towering peak was once beyond human reach. Such height was believed to be the reserve for gods. Therefore Indian pilgrims regard the mountain as the embodiment of a god. The Tibetans regard the mountain as Goddess Snow. The mountain has thus gained a sacred quality and many enchanting myths. One Tibetan myth goes like this: the Himalaya region was once an expanse of ocean with an unending stretch of forest on the coast, a haven for all kinds of beasts and birds. Then suddenly came a gigantic five-headed demon from the sea, frightening away all the animals and disturbing the peace. However, the demon was soon subdued by five fairies who were turned from five clouds. They were asked to stay by the grateful animal kingdom and became five Himalaya peaks with one of them being Mt Qomolangma, also known as the Third Goddess.

Myths are beautiful, but Mount Qomolangma is awe-inspiring and spectacular. When you have experienced its fascination in person, the greatest being between heaven and earth, you will appreciate the tangible meaning of greatness. The absolute serenity, the potent force of life still in its prime youth after two million years, the etheral beauty of the changing scenes of a mountain at sunrise, the unexplicable myth and the brutal force of wildness are all presented in their stark barenss and elemental essence. Won't you want to experience what it means to exert physically and emotionally every step of your journey and the direct dialogue and confrontation with nature? Very likely you will. Then mark the best months of April through June for the journey.

Mount Qomolangma（Mt. Everest）and
Ronggbu Lamasery

81

Distant view of Mt. Qomolangma
Mt. Qomolangma in first rays of morning
sun（8846.27m）

▷ Peaks of Himalayas

▷ Mt. Qomolangma in evening glow

▷ Scripture banners and Mt. Qomolangma

Forest of serac

Ice mushrooms

Icecles

Glacier

Mound formed through freezing and expanding

Plants on the eastern slope

Plants on the eastern slope

Plants on the eastern slope

Snow lotus（Saussurea involucrata）on Himalayas

A Girl of Menba nationality

Eagle of Mt. Qomolangma

Blue sheep

A man of Menba nationality

85

VIII. Tour in Ngari (I)
— Climbing up Roof of the World's Roof

Further west from Xigaze and beyond the Yarlung Zhangbo River near Gyangze, the land contour is elevated gradually. Turning toward north at No. 22 Road Maintenance Station and driving past the Dagyaco Lake, the traveller will be on his road into the Ngari highland.

The Tibetan Plateau has often been described as the Roof of the World which rises majestically toward the west in the region of Ngari, known as the top of Roof of the World. In a vast region of about 300,000 square kilometers are the towering northern Tibet highland, majestic mountain ranges of Gangdisê, Kunlun and Himalaya, and a great number of treacherous canyons, picturesque valleys, rivers and lakes. Expansive stretches of highland pasture, precipitous mountains, placid lakes and swift rivers against a backdrop of azure skies and floating clouds are absolutely exhilarating.

Driving along the central tour route via Coqin from Lhaze to the town of Shiquanhe(Sênggê grong), the regional center of Ngari, one will have wonderful views of the golden cone-shaped peak of the Shanmubati Mountain, the vast Zari Namco Lake and its island of bird haven, the Dawaco Lake with lush green banks and the snow-capped peaks of the Balinggangri mountain. The road to Shiquanhe begins at Lhasa and passes through Nagqu in the vast pasture area. Travelling in the highland region, one will see changing sights of spectacular scenery and rich wild life including beavers, rabbits and foxes not far from roadside, wild ducks, black-necked cranes and a variety of birds by the lake-side and antelopes, wild donkeys on more distant hills. North of Gerzê is the uninhabited zone of Lugu which is the domain of wild yaks and bears.

Ngari is easily accessible by road. The road from Yecheng of Xinjiang to Burang passes through Ngari. Lhaze-Burang road forms the southern route. The former has been known as the road with the highest elevation in the world and winds through the Kunlun mountains at 5,406 meters above sea level. The Bangongco Lake in northern Ngari has a surface elevation of 4,241 meters and a depths of 41.3 meters. This oblong lake extends 150 kilometers and is 50 meters at its narrowest. The lake water becomes salty in the western end. The lake is ringed by fertile pastures and has a few small islands that are haven for migratory birds including spotted wild geese, which often number in tens of thousands in the summer time. The monastery and cliff drawings found near Rutog and the uninhabited land in northern Tibet hold special appeal to explorers. The town of Shiquanhe (Sênggê grong) with an elevation of 4,300 meters is a newly risen center on the bank of the river Shiquanhe (Sênggê Zangbo). The Ngari Prefecture not only has spectacular scenery and an exotic local tradition but also occupies an important place in Tibetan history and the history of Buddhism. The secluded Guge ruins and the holy mountains and lakes in the region are sources of unending enchantment to tourists.

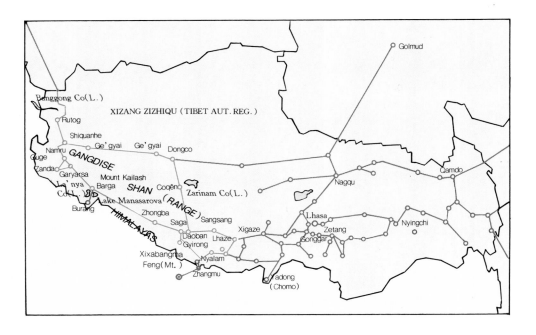

Landscape of northern slope of Mt Balingangri

Before rainstorm

Ngari Plateau after snow fall in July
Grazing land by Sênggê Zangbo

Buddhist dagoba in the glow of setting sun

Father and son travelling on the plateau

Altitude, Atmosphere, Air Density and Boiling Point

Alititude (meter)	Atmospheric Pressure (mb)	Air Density (g/m³)	Oxygen Content		Boiling Point (℃)
			g/m³	Compared with that of sea level (%)	
7000	420	573	133	47	77
6000	481	644	149	52	80
5000	549	719	166	59	84
4000	624	802	186	65	87
3000	707	892	206	73	90
0	1013.2	1292	260	100	100

Beautiful Northern Tibet Plateau

Mongolian gazelles   Tibetan wild donkeys

Golden dunes

Black-neck cranes on Dawatso Lakeside

Red willow on the plateau

Solar Energy Power Station of Gertsê
County

A Tibetan girl

Panorama of Shiquanhe Town（Sênggê grong）

A Tibetan pupil

A man of Gegyai

Geothermal energy resources of Langjiu

Herdsgirls

Tibetan women of Shiquanhe

Men of Ngari

An old woman

◁ Evening glow over Bangong Lake
Bird Island on Bangong Lake
Birds hovering over the lake

Newly-hatched birds

May on Bird Island

Moon-lit Bangong Lake

Morning on the lakeside

Swamp where water birds inhabit

Wild donkeys in depopulated region of
Northern Tibet

Camping site on Northern Tibet Plateau

Making scientific investigation on lakes
of Northern Tibet Plateau

Three dagobas of different colours at
Rutog

Sculptured roc behind statue of Buddha

Sculptured stone on mane pile

Rock painting

IX. Tour in Ngari (2)
— Ruins of Mystic Guge Kingdom

According to Tibetan historical annals, after the sudden death of Tsampo Langdama, the last king of the Tubo Kingdom, in the wake of his persecution of Buddhists, his two rival sons, Yundan and Osong, were locked in a bloody war for the throne which continued for two generations. Osong's son was killed by the soldiers of his rival kin and his two orphaned sons fled Lhasa. Jede, the elder of the two, took refuge in Ngari where he married the local chieftain's daughter who borne him three sons. The youngest had a son named Keri who became   founder of the Guge Kingdom whose territory once included all the farm and pasture land in southern Ngari. A hill of about 300 meters high stands to the south of Xiangquan River (Langqên Kanbab) in Zanda County. A complex of palaces, temples, fortifications, Buddhist pagodas and military tunnels right up the slope of the hill form the ruins of a lost kingdom. The construction began in the tenth century and was continuously expanded by 16 successive kings until the 16th century. These imposing buildings on the treacherous slope are connected by tunnels and protected by solid fortifications. The Kingdom of Guge played an important role in the rival of Tibetan Buddhism. The Guge kings were ardent advocates of the religion who sent envoys to India to invite Buddhist masters to Tibet and sponsored the translation of scriptures. The religious revival began in Ngari and extended to the entire Tibetan region. The kingdom also kept Tibet from repeated invasions by enemies from the west. A brutal battle in the 16th century brought the kingdom to an abrupt end. No writings can be found today about its fate there after and the ruins are the only evidence of the once majestic palaces and crushed glory.

As the visitor climbs up the hill slope, he can easily see the ruins of block houses, spacious palaces and glorious temples everywhere. The remains of painted sculptures and frescoes stand testimony to an art tradition that claimed splendor and diversity. The wealth of artifacts sealed stories of kings, ministers, clergymen and common people in the lost era of grandeur.

Ruins of Palace of Guge Kingdom

Ruins of Tolin Temple

▷ Bell chimes

▷ Two crows on an ancient dagoba

Langqên Kanbab
(Xiangquan River)
in evening glow

Viewing Himalayas from north

Scenery of Zanda

Distant view of Ruins of Guge Imperial Palace

Wall with sculptured mane stones

Ruins of ancient dagobas

Mane stone with sculpture of Buddha

Mural in Grand Weide Hall

Mane stone with sculpture of Buddha

Mural in Zhuoma （Goddess） Hall： Wedding Ceremony，Entertainment

108

Wooden pillars in White Hall

Tunnel in the ruins of Imperial Palace

Ancient knife, helmet, armor and shield

Blockhouses on the periphery of Imperial Palace

Mural in Red Hall

Statue in White Hall

Mural in Red Hall

Mural in Red Hall：Subduing Demons　　　　　　　　　　Mural in Hall of Mandala
Mural in Hall of Mandala　　　　　　　　　　　　　　　　Mural in Hall of Mandala

X. Tour in Ngari (3)
— The Holy Mountain and Sacred Lake

According to ancient Sanskrit documents, the Gangdisê Range had become a holy mountain as early as 2,000 years before Christ. The Hindu myth has it that the "palace" for the god of gods was built on the peak of Kailash of the Gangdisê Range. This important mountain in Asian history with elevation of 6,656 meters is located in the county of Burang in Ngari area. The Tibetan Buddhists believe that the mountain is in the shape of an olive with a grand legendary palace on the peak. Four streams flow down the mountain from four sources, each in the shape of a horse, lion, elephant and peacock which have given names to the four famous rivers in Ngari. The mountain top "palace" was home to 500 arhats. It is believed that centuries ago a visiting Bangladesh monk had heard chimes of bells and drum beats from the "Palace". Pilgrims today still claim that a few lucky ones may hear mysterious sounds from the mountain. Kailash crowns the Himalayan mountains with its myriad of myths and legends and remains the focus of the religious emotions of those who feel its pull. For centuries, pilgrims have come from afar to pay homage, praying for redemption by walking around this holy mountain of purity and benevolence. A full circle around the mountain takes from 24 hours to 36 hours. This tradition of worshipping was deep rooted in ancient pagan rituals and is still alive and strong today. One myth has it that Mila Xiba, a famous Tibetan monk, subdued a heretic in battle of faith and power on Mt Kailash. The victory has been celebrated in every Year of the Horse when pilgrimage to the holy mountain is at its height.

Lake Manasarova, one of the highest fresh water lakes of the world, is over 20 km to the southeast of Mount Kailash with a total surface area of 400 square kilometers. This placid lake is a vast expanse of pristine water, absolutely beautiful under the vast and clear sky. The legend has it that Goddess Woma bathed in the lake. Because of its sheer beauty and charming myths and legends, the lake was mentioned as a celestial lake of the west in an ancient book written by Xuan Zhuang, a Tang dynasty monk known for his journey to India in search of Buddhist scriptures. The book was entitled "The Western Territories of the Great Tang Empire". The lake was already known to the Tibetans as Macuico about nine centuries ago. It was believed that in the "palace of the dragon king" on the bottom of the lake were bondless treasures. The chosen ones after walking around the lake a full circle would be promised a life of plenty by a small fish, a pebble or a feather they might have picked up. After the triumphant rise of Buddhism in Tibet in the 11th century, the lake was given a Buddhist name "Manasarova", meaning "perpetually invincible". Thereafter, the lake has been regarded as a gift from Buddha with cleansing and redeeming power that will bring spiritual and physical well-being. The lake has thus gained a primordial force which, together with the Holy Mountain Kailash, has attracted countless pilgrims to the area of Ngari. They would take the strenuous journey around the mountain and lake as a test of their faith and for an experience of the holy power. Many of them have harbored the wish of bathing in the lake for many years. There are four holy bathing spots around the lake respectively named Lotus, Fragrance, Purification and Faith. Bathing at each spot while trekking around the lake would redeem different sins. The mysterious powers of Lake Manasarova are believed to be just as great as those of the towering Mount Kailash.

Holy Mountain in evening glow

Holy Mountain — Mt. Kailash（6656 m）

Northern side of Mt Kailash

Scripture streamers

▷ Valley on the western side of the mountain

Devout pilgrims

Remains of competition site of religeous
power in religious legend

Foreign pilgrims

Jomala Pass above 5700 meters

A small lake on high mountain

Mt Neimona'nyi and Sacred Lake in evening glow

Camping site at the foot of Holy Mountain

◁ Spiritual pilgrimage
◁ Monks and lamas from afar
◁ Praying for the best
Praying in evening glow

Holy Mountain Kailash and Sacred
Lake Manasarova

Water of Sacred Lake

◁ Sacred Lake at dawn
  Jiwusi Lamasery
▷ Chuguosi Lamasery

XI. Travel Along Great Valleys Between the Himalayas and Gangdisê Ranges—From Shiquanhe to Zhangmu

The majestic Himalaya Range on the southwestern periphery of the massive Qinghai-Tibetan Plateau extends over 2,400 kilometers. The Gangdisê Range lies to its northeast in an almost parallel direction. Between the two mountain ranges lie the Shiquan River (Sênggê Zangbo) valley, Ge'er Zhangbo River valley and a number of smaller or bigger valleys with average elevations between 4,250 and 4,400 meters. The source of the Yarlung Zhangbo River, the highest among all world's major rivers, is the Jema Yangzhong Glaciers on the northern slope of Himalayas and the river flows eastward in the valley between the two mountain ranges. Highland pastures spread along the valleys.

Travelling from the town of Shiquanhe (Sênggê grong) to Zhangmu along the southern route stretching through the valleys between the two mountain ranges is a most exhilarating experience. Towering snow-capped mountains lie along the road for hundreds of kilometers, presenting scenery of breath-taking beauty. The landscape along the route changes from highland pasture to desolate sandy stretches, lush marshes, lakes, rivers, mountain forests and waterfalls.

The highland weather can be tempestuous. Clear azure skies can be blackened by thick clouds with rain or even hail all of a sudden and clear up again with a bright rainbow. Even in the summer month of August, overnight snow may shroud the landscape in white. The highland scenery is at its best in the early morning or at dusk with purple colored clouds and fiery snow peaks reflecting the setting sun. Startled rabbits, beavers, eagles and antelopes are here and gone in no time. Only intrepid wild donkeys will gallop along with the intruding vehicles in the quietness of the mountain valley. At Jelong Valley, long-tailed monkeys and blue sheep can sometimes be spotted.

The local traditions and traditional dresses vary for the regions of Ge'er, Zanda, Burang, Zhongba, Jelong and Zhangmu. Their temples and monasteries also show unique styles. The valley region is rich in historical heritage in addition to being an ancient trading route. The Guge ruins in Zanda, the holy Kailash Mountain and Manasarova Lake in Burang County are of historical and religious significance, which attract an endless stream of visitors and pilgrims.

The remote town of Burang is an oasis at the foot of the harsh and domineering Himalayas. Its ancient history, primitive life style, spectacular mountains and canyons and unique location hold eternal fascination to travellers, pilgrims, scholars and itinerant vendors. The town is also a border trading post with a number of roads extending through the Himalayas to Nepal and India.

Travelling along a route accompanied by the great mountain ranges of Himalaya and Gangdisê, the traveller will experience the breath-taking grandeur and beauty of nature on the Roof of the World, the vigor of a primitive life of highland people and the mystery of sacred places of Buddhism. It will be truly an unforgettable experience.

Ngari Plateau in summer

Distant view of Holy Mountain at dusk

Auspitious journey

Ge'er Grazing Land in evening glow

Travellers on plateau

Moincer Spring

▷ Evening glow over Kongqi River

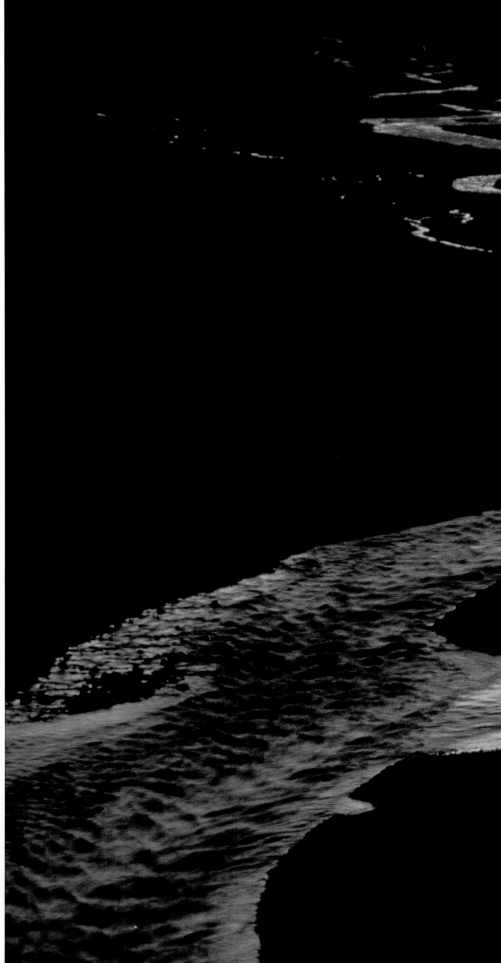

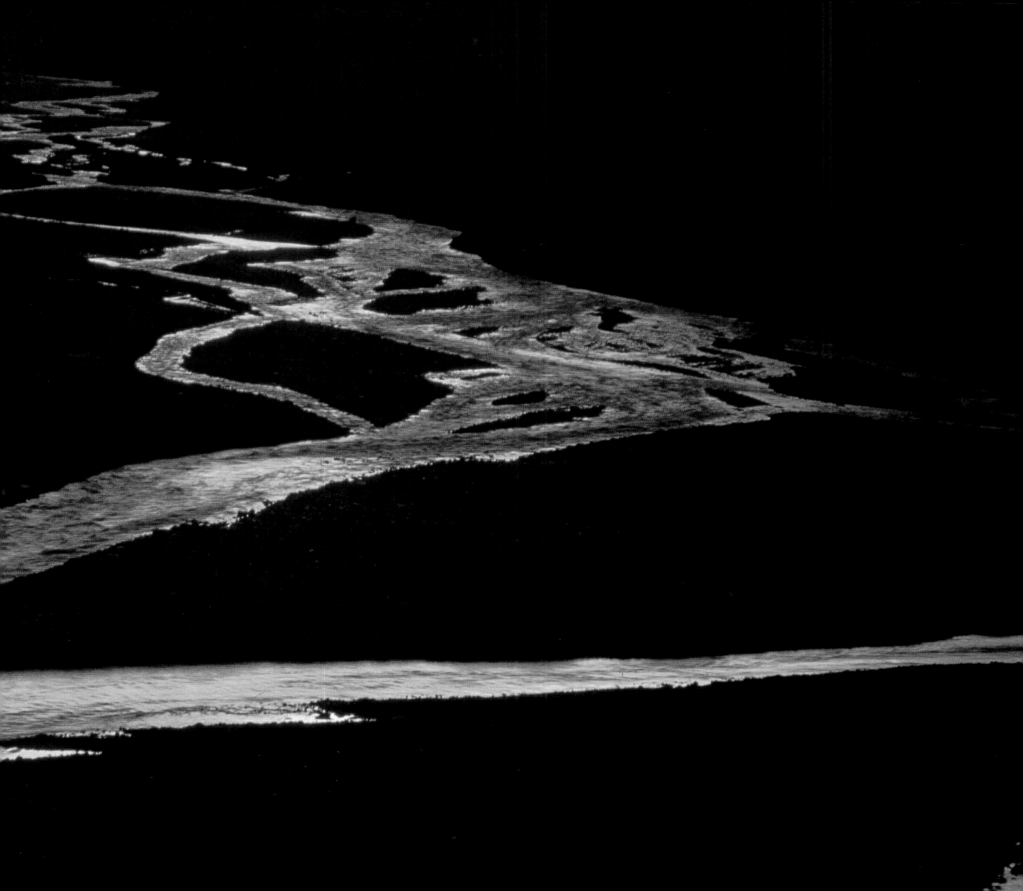

A village at the foot of Himalayas

Mt. Neimona'nyi at dawn

Awakening mountains

Distant view of peaks of Himalayas

Lake Lha'angtso

▷ Beautiful Mount Kangciren

Turning scripture wheels

Panorama of Burang County Town

Remains of ancient palace

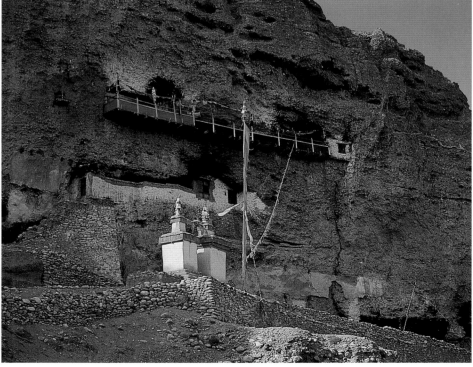

Burang women in Sunday dress

Scripture-turning Path outside Korchag
Lamasery
Ancient Korchag Lamasery

The Himalayas at dawn
Plateau at dusk

On the way of pilgrimaging

Women on a long journey of pilgrimaging

Trade caravan on the plateau

Driving across a stream

Picnicking

Passing the desert

Camping site at the foot of the snow-clad mountain

Crossing Yarlung Zangbo River

Camping by Damgo Kanbab（Maquan River）

Camping on lakeside

Glacier at the source of Yarlung
Zangbo River

Grazing land on plateau in summer

▷ In evening glow

Wild plants（1—6）

Wild donkeys racing with cars

Red flowers on Gobi Desert   Lake Peikutso

◁ Mount Nantankangri
Ancient temple at Gyirong

Blue sheep

Cliff sculpture

Langurs

Rhesus monkeys

143

◁ Mt. Shishabangma and Lake Peikutso
Main peak of Mt. Shishabangma（8012m）
Scenery on southern slope of Himalayas
Streams on southern slope of Himalayas
Yaruxiongla Pass
Zhangmu Town

145

XII. Mountaineering Tour in Tibet, China

After mankind conquered both the Antarctic and Arctic in the 20th century, explorers turned their attention to the Tibetan Plateau. For millenia this land of majestic mountains was shrouded in mystery and beyond the reach of most aspiring mountaineers except for a select few.

Beginning from the 1980s, Tibet was no longer just gilded pinnacles, monasteries, historical anecdotes and myths to outside visitors. The towering mountains of Tibet are popular with mountaineers who wish to test their strength and spirit and transcend the limits imposed by nature on human endeavor. The Tibetan Plateau has an average altitude of over 4,000 meters with many world-famous mountain ranges renowned for their elevation, relative young age and spectacular sceneries. In the Himalayan Range alone, there are over 50 peaks with elevations of more than 7,000 meters and 11 peaks 8,000 meters. Mountaineering or trekking along secluded mountain trails will create better than anything else a heightened sense of self-awareness and transcendence. In the absolute wildness, you are one with Nature, an exhilerating experience that you will never get anywhere else. There are many mountain peaks in Tibetan Plateau that remain untouched by man's foot steps. The 7,782-meter Namjagbawa Peak was once the highest yet to be scaled by man. The face of the peak was so steep that efforts by a team of Chinese and Japanese mountaineers in 1991 ended in failure with a number of deaths. But this did not stop another team of Chinese and Japanese climbers who conquered this virgin peak in October, 1992 with 11 of them reaching the top. The "Roof of the World" is world of mountains which pose ever changing challenges to mountaineers who always want to scale new heights or climb mountains that have been climbed before by different routes. In recent years, the region has sponsored programs such as multi-national joint climbing, straight line approach, climbing without oxygen supplies, speed climb and solitary climb. Difficult approaches and harsh climate have been chosen to test the extreme limits of human endurance.

In order to accommodate the needs of mountaineers from around the world, a total of 44 mountain peaks have been open to international climbers since 1980. As people are eager to return to the embrace of nature, mountaineering, highland exploration and trekking in the Tibetan Plateau will become increasingly popular as a retreat into Nature.

Evening glow over Mt. Qomolangma

Banner cloud over Mt. Qomolangma

▷ Mount Nyainqentanglha （7117m）

Mount Cho Oyu （8201m）

Precipitous snow-clad peaks

▷ ▷ Third Goddess （Mt Qomolangma）

◁ ◁ Mount Langbokangri

◁ Mount Namjagbawa

◁ Mount Zalasongo

Golden peak

Mt. Xixabangma in first rays of dawn

Striding over icy stream

Base camp of a Mt. Qomolangma mountaineering expedition

Aiming at the highest peak

Climbing cliff

On the summit of Mt. Namjagbawa

PEAKS OPEN FOR MOUNTAINEERING (44)

Name of Peak	Altitude(m)	Position	Name of Peak	Altitude(m)	Position
Mt. Qomolangma	8846.27	Tingri	Mt. Nyanchen Thanglha	7117	Damshung
Mt. Lhotse	8516	Tingri	Mt. Norbu Gangri	7095	Dongpa
Mt. Makalu	8463	Tingri	Mt. Lixin	7071	Tingri
Mt. Qowowuyag	8201	Tingri	Mt. Jiegang Susong	7060	Nakartse
Mt. Shisha Pangma	8012	Nyalam	Mt. Kanggeduo	7060	Tsona
Mt. Gezhongkang	7985	Tingri	Mt. Chowusha Jianzi	7022	Tingri
Mt. Molamenqing	7703	Nyalam	Mt. Qiageru	7021	Tingri
Mt. Nemo Nanyi	7694	Purang	Mt. Xiangdong	7018	Tingri
Mt. Zhangzi	7543	Tingri	Mt. Balung	7013	Tingri
Mt. Kulagangri	7538	Lhodak	Mt. Xiakangjian	6822	Tsochen
Mt. Labuchikang	7367	Tingri	Mt. Gela Gangri	6666	Nyalam
Mt. Qiaoniaoyi	7351	Tingri	Mt. Samding Gangsing	6590	Nakchu
Mt. Siguang	7308	Tingri	Mt. Donakposang	6587	Tingri
Mt. Xifeng	7292	Nyalam	Mt. Namtsori	6536	Tingri
Mt. Kangboqin	7281	Nyalam	Mt. Tsanglha	6495	Nyalam
Mt. Khadhaphu	7227	Tingri	Mt. Lhago Gangri	6457	Lhatse
Mt. Nojin Gangsang	7206	Nakartse	Mt. Puleri	6404	Tingri
Mt. Nadhangri	7205	Nyalam	Mt. Jiangsanglamu	6324	Nakartse
Mt. Menlongze	7175	Tingri	Mt. Qizi	6206	Damshung
Mt. Phumari	7170	Tingri	Mt. Luktse	6154	Damshung
Mt. Jialabailei	7151	Miling	Mt. Xiemaguo	6140	Nyemo
Mt. Tashi Tseringma	7134	Tingri	Mt. Khadhajopho	6112	Nyemo

XIII. Joyous Traditional Festivals

The most colorful and electrifying things in Tibet are its many traditional and exotic festivals which spread throughout the year with one or two of some kind for each month. These festive dates have their origins rooted in folk traditions, religious celebration or traditional activities. The festivals are often rituals, farming events, commemerations, celebrations, social gatherings or simple amusement, which reflect the historical roots of the Tibetan ethnic people, their religious belief and closeness to Nature.

The Festival of Banishing Evils falls on December 29 on the Tibetan calendar. Similar expressions are found in ethnic celebrations around the world with a theme of driving away evil spirits. On that day, a sorcerer's dance is performed in monasteries and a general cleaning is done in every household to get rid of misfortune and pray for godly blessings. Every family will have a traditional New Year's Eve dinner of Guthuk and torches are lit and howlings are heard everywhere in a collective prayer for a new year free from misfortunes.

On the Tibetan New Year's Day, each home will open its doors with prayers and fetch the first bucket of water of the year. People will greet each other with well-meaning wishes. This is the most important festival for the Tibetans, during which they entertain themselves with various folk activities such as wrestling, weight throwing, tug-of-war and horse-racing.

The Great Prayer Festival, from January 8 through 14 on the Tibetan calendar, is the grandest religious festival in Tibet. It has its origin in a prayer meeting organized at Johhang Temple by Tsong Khapa, founder of the Gelukpa Sect, in 1409. Thousands of monks from far and near will gather for prayers, theological debates and examination for Geshe, a doctoral degree in Buddhist theology, at the temple. Pilgrims will come from everywhere to listen to sermons.

The Butter Lamp Festival falls on January 15 of the Tibetan calendar, which has its origin in a celebration with many butter lamps to honor the victory of Sakyamuni in a debate against Heretics. During the festive celebration, Barkor Street in Lhasa is crowded with people and by nightfall is brightly lit with thousands of lamps made of butter in an intriguing assortment of designs. The festive mood lasts throughout the night.

Saga Dawa Festival on April 15 marks the birth, transcendence and death of Sakyamuni. Pilgrims and secular folks will visit Lhasa and the festival is observed by turning prayer wheels, having vegetarian lunch and a picnic by the Dragon King Pond. Folk entertainers will perform Tibetan music and traditional operas. According to Tibetan tradition, they will pay their homage to Buddha, observe a vegetarian rule, refrain from killing domestic animals and give out alms during the month.

Gyangtse Horse-race Festival. Archery contests on horseback are popular throughout the Tibetan region. It became events on fixed dates in 1408 when the king of Gyangze gave a decree marking the period from April 10 through 27 of every year for prayers and sacrifical ceremony for his grandfather with entertainment offered on the 28th. By the mid-17th century, original ritual ceremonies became symbolic and contests of archery on horseback grew to be the most important events for the festival. Nowadays, with all kinds of entertainment and fairs organized it has become one of the most important festivals in Tibet.

The Shoton Festival is one of the grandest festivals in Tibet. Prior to the 17th century, Shoton had been an exclusively religious observance. The month of June on the Tibetan calendar was reserved for self-cultivation and meditation for all the monks who were not allowed to go out of monasteries until July 1, when local residents would offer alms of yoghurt (Sho, in Tibetan). From around the mid-17th century, Tibetan local operas were added to festival celebrations which were held around monasteries and in Lhasa the Drepung Monastery. From the beginning of the 18th century, the main site of the festival was moved to Norbu Lingka and celebrations became formalized which include shining of the Buddha's portrait, folk amusement at the local park and performances of Tibetan operas. Popular fairs are also organized during the festival.

For a whole week in early July when Venus appears in the sky every year, Tibetans will bathe themselves all day long in rivers across the region, believing that bathing may cure illness and get rid of misfortune at a time when water is purest and mildest.

According to a Tibetan myth, the gods will descend from the Heaven on the 22nd of the ninth month of the Tibetan calendar every year. All monasteries will be open on this day to the needy and prayers and sutra chants will be given.

Tsong Khapa's Festival, falling on the 25th of the tenth month of the Tibetan calendar, marks the anniversary of the passing away of Tsong Khapa, the founder of Gelukpa Sect, and is called Ganden Angchuin in Tibetan. On this day, butter lamps are placed on the roofs of monasteries and secular homes and sutras are chanted in praise of Tsong Khapa.

Guoshe Dance of the grassland

Great Prayer Festival

Leading a scripture chanting

Blowing conch

Order keeping lama

Guards of Honour

◁ Incantation-chanting Monk in Helmet Dance
Butter Lamp show
Tired.

157

Meidojoba (Offering Flower) Dance

Dance of Buddha's Warrior Attendants

Black Helmet Dance

Sagadawa (April) Festival

Unfolding portrait of Buddha at Potala Palace

At the eve of festival

Unfolding Buddha at Tashilhunpo
Monastery

▷ Giant portrait of Buddha

▷ Unfolding portrait of Buddha at
Drepung Monastery

▷ Buddha-unfolding procession

Yak racing

An expert archer

Picking up hada

Tug-of-war

Archers

Tibetan opera actors
Tibetan opera actresses
Masks in Tibetan opera

A folk artist
▷ Fairies in Tibetan opera

Ga'er Dance at Sakya Lamasery

Reba Dance

A dance-leading old man

Dance of Rezhen Lamasery

A Tibetan woman

Before the performance

Tibetan opera "Jowasamu"

Cavaliers in ancient tunic at Onkor (Harvest) Festival

Tibetan actresses

Norbu Lingka at festival

Bathing Festival

In deep thought

Dressed up as warriors

▷ Festival offerings at Rezhen Lamasery

DATES OF TIBETAN TRADITIONAL FESTIVALS

FESTIVAL	Time						INTRODUCTION
	1995	1996	1997	1998	1999	2000	
Tibetan New Year	2 Mar	19 Feb	8 Feb	7 Feb	17 Feb	6 Feb	It is the greatest festival in Tibet. In ancient times when the peach tree was in blossom it was considered as the starting of a new year. Since the systematization of the Tibetan calendar in 1027 A.D., the first day of the first month has become fixed as the New Year. On the New Year's Day, families unite, "auspicious dipper" is offered, and the auspicious words "tashi delek" are greeted.
Great Prayer Festival	9—15 Mar	21 Feb —6 Mar	10—25 Feb	1—15 Mar	19 Feb— 5 Mar	8—21 Feb	It is the greatest religious festival in Tibet. Instituted by Tsong Khapa in 1409, the founder of the Gelukpa sect. Monks from the Three Great Monasteries of Tibet assemble in Jokhang for pray to Shakyamumni's image as if it were the living Buddha. Philosophical debates are held among candidates for the Doctor of Metaphysics. Pilgrims come from every corner of Tibet and donations are offered to monks.
Butter —Lamp	16 Mar	5 Mar	22 Feb	21 Mar	2 Mar	19 Feb	It is the last day of the Great Prayer Festival. In order to celebrate Shakyamuni's victory over non—Buddhist opponents, the Lord of Neu Dzong, a noted patron of Tsong Khapa, illuminated numerous butter—lamps in 1409. Ever since the festival flourished.
Gyantse Horse Race and Archery	15—19 Jun	4—18 Jun	25 May— 8 Jun	13—27 Jun	2—16 Jun	19 Jun— 3Jul	Horse race and archery are generally popular in Tibet, and Gyantse enjoys prestige of being the earliest in history by starting in 1408. Contests in early times included horse race, archery, and shooting on gallop followed by a few days' entertainment or picnicking. Presently, ball games, track and field events, folk songs and dances, barter trade are in addition to the above.
The World Incense Day	12 Jul	1 Jul	20 Jun	9 Jul	28 Jun	16 Jul	Gods in heaven are believed to descend to the mortal world on this day. Incense is burnt in large scales and picnicking is done in public parks.
Six—Four Festival	31 Jul	19 Jul	7 Aug	26 Jul	16 Jul	3 Aug	It is believed the Buddha gave his first sermon on this day. People celebrate the festival by paying visits to the holy mountains.
"Shoton" Festival	26—30 Aug	14—30 Aug	1—7 Sep	22—28 Aug	11—25 Aug	29 Aug— 4 Sep	It is the Opera Festival and the greatest of festivals in Tibet. In ancient times pious folks went into mountain hermitages to do penance, and on the last day of which yoghort was served for meal followed by entertainments of folk songs and dances. Since 7th century, opera performances were held for days in Norbu Lingka. Presently, opera contests and distribution of prizes are held for seven days.
Bathing Week							It is believed when the sacred planet Venus appears in the sky the water in the river becomes purest and can cure diseases. During its appearance for one week in the sky all townspeople in Lhasa go into the river for bathing.
Death of Tsong Khapa	17 Dec						Tsong Khapa, the great reformer of Tibetan Buddhism and founder of the Gelukpa sect, died on this day in 1419. In memory of the day every household burns countless butter lamps on roof-tops and chant prayers in his honour. Late in the evening Tibetan dumpling is served for supper.
Driving off Evil Spirits	28 Feb	18 Feb	6 Jan	25 Feb	15 Feb	4 Feb	At the eve of Tibetan New Year, 29th of the twelveth month religious dances are per formed in monasteries for driving off evil spirits of the past year. At night in every household traditional means of driving off evil spirits is carried on by burning bundles of straws and throwing rubbish on crossroad. "Year—end dumpling" is served for supper.

XIV. Tibet — A Favorite Tourist Destination

Regular flights of Boeing 757 jets arrive at Gonggar Airport in the morning. After taxing on the 3,700-meter runway, the plane discharges passengers coming from different parts of the world, who are escorted by local tour guides to Lhasa on tourist coaches. So begins a traveller's adventure on the Roof of the World.

Since the policy of reform and opening to the outside world began to take effect in China, tourism industry in Tibet has experienced a boom as the region enjoys stability and ethnic harmony and its economy grows. A visitor to Tibet will easily find good tourist hotels and restaurants in almost every major town in the region linked by a network of well-maintained roads. Vehicles in good conditions and convenient service facilities are readily available and well-trained tour guides help make travel in the region a pleasant experience. The towns and villages in this highland region will give the traveller a feel of primitive simplicity and vigor mingled with elements of the contemporary world. The industrious and down-to-earth people of Tibet are hospitable. The exotic buttered-tea with a strong and pleasant aroma is relaxing and leaves an unforgettable after taste. The plateau is shrouded in profound religious mystery, attracting pilgrims from near and afar. The magnificent temples and monasteries, with lavishly adorned sculptures of Buddha and a great wealth of artifacts, have in them endless tales of the sacred past. The perpetual prayers conducted by the monks prompt soul-searching.

The spectacular highland landscape and majestic scenery are ever awe-inspiring. A variety of tours including cultural sight-seeing tours, trekking, scientific exploration and mountaineering are available to meet the needs of different visitors.

The exquisitely crafted artifacts are popular with tourists, too. Tibetan rugs, coasters, wooden bowls, daggers and colorful ornaments are ideal momentos. The Barkhor Street outside the Jokhang Temple and the local street market are a must for visitors to Lhasa, where they may derive great delight from getting a few goodies at bargain prices.

Then there are the festivals. Even in the depth of winter, the Tibetan New Year, the Grand Prayer Ceremony and Butter Lamp Festival will cheer up the spirit of the most solitary soul.

The Tibetan people are good dancers and singers. Their exotic music and dance vary from region to region. It is a rare experience to be entertained on the Roof of the World by dances and songs not seen or heard anywhere else.

With the growth of local economy, tourist facilities in Tibet have been upgraded. Improved telephone service offers direct dialing within China and internationally. Good medical services are also available. Direct domestic and international flights in and out of Lhasa have made the city a hub for the region.

Tibetan Autonomous Region welcomes visitors from around the world. Now that you know about their traditional buttered tea and the white Hada ribbons for honored guests, come and experience all the exhilaration and enchantment in Tibet, a paradise for travellers.

Celebrating birthday in Lhasa

Holiday Inn Lhasa

Lobby of Holiday Inn Lhasa

Wishing the guest a happy birthday

Guest room in Holiday Inn Lhasa

Tibetan-style Restaurant in Holiday Inn Lhasa

Tibet Hotel Lhasa
Xuelian Hotel
Plateau Hotel

Cafeteria in Tibet Hotel
Welcome Hotel
Kada Hotel

Tibetan-style guest room in Tibet Hotel
Snow Land Hotel
Autonomous Region Government Restaurant

Yak Hotel

Gyire Hotel

Shigatse Hotel

Sunlight Hotel

Banakxul Hotel

Shiquanhe Hotel

Himalaya Hotel

Tsetang Hotel

Nakchu Hotel

Tents in Kailash Hotel

Motorcade of Tourist Car Company

Lhasa Long-Distance Bus Station

Zhasongcuo Lake Holiday Resort

Visiting Drepung Monastery Tour

Ancient Palace Dance

Religious music

Tangka Stall

Foreign tourists going shopping

Arts and crafts stall

Women folk dance

Pedicabs in Lhasa

Stall of Religious Neccesities

Tibet Hotel Chengdu
Lhasa Gongkar Airport

Altitudes at Some Mountain Passes Along Toruist Highways in Tibet

Name of Pass	Altitude(meter)	Location	Name of Pass	Altitude(metre)	Location
Jieshandaban	5406	Yecheng—Rutok	Lalonglha Pass	5124	Tingri—Nyalam
Thanglha Pass	5206	Golmud—Amdo	Qielha	4926	Sangsang—22Daoban
Tou'erjiu Pass	5040	Thanglha—Amdo	Mangxionglha Pass	5000	Maizhokunggar—Kongpo Gymda
Jiuzilha	4444	Amdo—Yangpachen	Yasanglha Pass	4750	Tsetang—Tsome
Xuegulha Pass	5454	Yangpachen—Dazhuben	Seqilha Pass	4515	Nyingtri—Tangmai
Donggulha Pass	4960	Nyemo	Gangbalha Pass	4794	Nakartse
Damuyelha Pass	5013	Nakchu—Biru	Zhazhalha	4824	Kyirong
Jiatsolha Pass	5252	Shigatse—Lhatse			

Schedule of Flights from Lhasa to Chengdu, Chongqing and Kathmandu

Air Route	A/C	Days(week)	Dep	Arr	R
Lhasa/Chengdu	B757	(1)(2)(3)(4)(5)(6)(7)	09:40	11:20	
Lhasa/Chengdu	B757	(1)(2)(3)(4)(5)(6)(7)	09:50	11:40	
Lhasa/Chongqing	B757	(2)(5)	09:30	12:30	Effective from 1994, July 1st
Lhasa/Beijing	B757	(7)	09:50	14:15	via Chengdu
Lhasa/Kathmandu	B757	(2)(6)	10:20	11:30	

Major Tour Activities in Tibet

Lhasa Prefecture

Name	Location	Distance (km)	Activities
Potala Palace	Downtown		Sightseeing
Jokhang Lamasery	Old City		Sightseeing
Drepung Lamasery	West Suburbs	10	Sightseeing
Sera Temple	North Suburbs	8	Sightseeing
Norbu Lingka	Downtown		Sightseeing
Ramoche Temple	Old city		Sightseeing
	Northeast of the City	75	Sightseeing
Nunnery	Old City		Sightseeing
Naiqiong Temple	West Suburbs		Sightseeing
Local Family Visit	Downtown		Tibetan customs
Tibetan Medicine Hospial	Down town		Traditional Tibetan Medicine
Art School	Downtown		Tibetan Singing & Dance Show
Tibet University	Downtown		Education in Tibet
Barkhor Street	Old City		Sightseeing & shopping
Carpet Factory	Downtown		Visit & shopping
Yak — hide boat	Lhasa River		River crossing
Yamdok Tso Lake	Southwest of the City	130	Sightseeing of the Lake and snow mountain
Yangpanche's Terrestrial Heat	Northwest of the City	110	terrestrial heat and view of the snow — capped mountains
Tsongjiaolukang	Downtown		picnic & farmers' market

Nyingtri Prefecture

Name	Location	Distance (km)	Activities
Lake Basong Tso	Kongpo Gymda County		Sightseeing of the beautiful view of lakes and mountains
Mt. Namjagbawa	Nyingtri County		View of the snow mountain peaks
Bayi Town Scenic Spots	Bayi Town		Scenery of southeast Tibet
Pujiu Lama Monastery	Southwest of Bayi Town	30	Sightseeing
Woolen Mill	Bayi Town		Visiting & shopping
Singing & Dancing Show	Bayi Town		Menba and Lhoba dances

Ngari Prefecture

Name	Location	Distance (km)	Activities
Holy Mt. Kailash	Purang County		Walking around the mountain
Sacred Lake Manasarova	Purang County		Sightseeing and bathing in the lake
Guge Ruins	Tsada County		Sightseeing
Wild Animals	Rutok County		Sightseeing

Shannan Prefecture

Name	Location	Distance (km)	Activities
Yumbu Lukhong	South of Tsetang	15	sightseeing
Graveyard of Tibetan Kings	Qonggyai County	38	sightseeing
Chamzhu Lamasery	South of Tsetang	10	sightseeing
Samye Lamasery	North of Yarlung Zangbo River	50	sighseeing
Zhegu Grassland	South of Tsetang	150	sightseeing grassland
City Tour	Downtown		Shopping & Sightseeing
Visit to a Local Family	Downtown		Life of the Tibetans
Evening Entertainment	Mass Art Center		Tibetan costumes show, singing & dancing show

Shigatse Prefecture

Name	Location	Distance (km)	Activities
Tashilhunpo Temple	downtown		sighseeing
Touring Palace of Panchen Lama	downtown		sightseeing
Shalu Monastery	southeast of the city	20	sightseeing
Tibetan Medicine Hospital	downtown		trditional Tibetan medicine
Visit to a Local Family	downtown		life in Rear Tibet
Farmers' Market	downtown		visiting & shopping
Sakya Temple	Sakya County	180	sightseeing
Mt. Qomolangma	Tingri County	240	Viewing the snow — clad peaks
Carpet Factory	downtown		shopping

Gyangtse Prefecture

Name	Location	Distance (km)	Activities
Baiju Lamasery Ten — Thousound Buddha Pogadas	in the town		sightseeing
Buddhist Nunnery	in the town		sightseeing
Carpet Factory	in the town		visiting & shopping

Nakchu Prefecture

Name	Location	Distance (km)	Activities
Nakchu Horse Race	Nakchu Town		hores-race
Xiaodeng Monastery	in the town		sightseeing
Visit to a local family	in the town		life of north Tibetan herdsmen
Local religion temple	Diru County		sightseeing
Wild animals	Palgon Lake		sightseeing
Qinghai — Tibet Plateau			grassland, snow — capped mountain peaks

Altitude (above sea-level) of Main Cities and Towns in Tibet Autonmous Region

City(Town)	Altitude(metre)
Amdo	4800
Nagqu	4507
Qamdo	3240
Damxung	4200
Bomi	2750
Lhasa	3658
Nyingchi	3000
Zetang	3500
Xigaze	3836
Gyangze	4040
Tingri	4300
Zayu	2327
Pagri	4300
Shiquanhe	4300
Burang	3700
Rutog	4250

Health Care For Travelling on Plateau

For the high altitude, thin air, cold and aridity of Tibet, travellers usually will have altitude sicknes of different degrees, such as headache, insomnia, feeling depressed and nervous. To cure these sicknesses, we would remind you to have enough rest and not to catch cold. For the light sick ones, medicine is not necessary but just rest. While for the seriouly sick, tours must be stopped immediately. The patients should lie down in bed and, if possible, they should inhale oxygen (Hotels can always provide oxygen bags and cylinders) Inhaling oxygen is a convenient and effective way of curing altitude sickness. To ensure a happy trip and good health, tourists are suggested to bring some common medicines for altitude sickness such as aminophyline, chlorpromazine, Asprin, Vitamin C, E, B_1, B_6, etc.

Seasons and Clothing

Because of its high altitude, climate in Tibet is somewhat cold and the difference between temperature in the day and at night is very great. But as for its long sunshine time, winter is not too bad. Its annual rainfall is not much and mostly come in between July and September. In spring, autumn and winter it is a little bit dry. In the river valleys there is not much snow.

Spring (March — May): Cold, dry and windy. A jacket and a woolen sweater are necessary.

Summer (June — August): Cool but hot at noon. Shirts, pants or skirts will be fine.

Autumn (Sep. — Nov.): Cold, dry. Jackets and woolen sweater are needed.

Winter (Dec. — Feb. next year): Frigid, very dry. Warm pullover, down coat, jacket, woolen sweater, scarves and gloves are necessary.

Major Tour Schedules in Tibet

Tour Route	Days	Means of Transport	Itinerary
Lhasa — Shigatse — Zhangmu	8	Motorcar	Potala Palace, Jokhang Lamasery, Tashilhunpo Temple, Baiju Temple, Tibetan Medicine Hospital, a visit to a local family. Mt. Qomolangma, Carpet Factory, Sakya Temple.
Lhasa — Tsetang (Shannan)	5	Motorcar	Potala Palce, Jokhang Lamasery, Yumbu Lukhang, Graveyard for Tibetan Kings, Chamzhu Lamasery, Samye Temple, a visit to a local family, Singing & Dance Show at night.
Lhasa — Lake Basongtso — Nyingtri — Gyatsa — Tsetang	10	Motorcar	Potala Palace, Jokhang Lamasery, Kongpo Gymda, Lake Basongtso, Mt. Namjagbawa, Sightseeing at Southeast Tibet, Ancient Graveyards at Lieshan Mountain, Yumbu Lukhang, Graveyard for Tibetan Kings, Chamzhu Lamasery, Singing & Dance Show.
Lhasa — Golmud	2 — 5	Motorcar	Grasslands, Snow Mountains, Wild Animals, Lake Namtso, Herdsmen's Life, Bonnist Temples, sources of Yangtze River and Yellow River.
Lhasa — Base Camps at Mt. Qomolangma	7	Motorcar, Horse, Trekking	Potala Palace, Jokhang Temple, Tashilhunpo Temple, Himalaya Mountains, Mt. Qomolangma, Horseriding, Walking.
Lhasa — Shigatse — Ngari (Mt. Kailash and Lake Manasarova)	over 15	Bus (Walking around Mt. Kailash and Lake Manasarova)	Potala Palace, Jokhang Palace, Tashilhunpo Temple, Wild Animals, Walking around Mt. Kailash, bathing in Lake Manasarova.
Gandan Monastery — Samye Monastery	3	Horse-riding, Walking	Horse-riding to Gandan Monastery, walking and picnic and camping, enjoying view of the lake and mountain, Samye Monastery, Yarlung Zangbo River.

Distance Between Major Cities in Tibet Autonomous Region

Terminal Cities	Distance (km)	Cities (Towns) Passing by
Lhasa — Golmud	1165	Yangpachen, Damxung, Nagqu, Amdo, Tanggula Shankou
Lhasa — Chengdu	2410	Mainzhokunggar, Gongbo Gyamda, Nyingchi, Bomi, Baxio, Bangda, Qamdo, Jomda, Jinsha River Bridge
Lhasa — Zhangmu	662	Yangpachen Xigaze, Gyangze, Tingri, Nyalam
Lhasa — Nagqu	317	Yangpachen, Damxung
Lhasa — Zetang	183	Gonggar
Lhasa — Nyingchi	420	Maizhokunggar, Gongboyamda
Lhasa — Xigaze (South Line)	345	Quxu, Nagarze, Gyangze
Lhasa — Xigaze (Middle Line)	228	Nyemo
Lhasa — Xigaze (North Line)	328	Yangpachen, Dagzhuka
Lhasa — Yadong	464	Quxu, Nagarze, Gyangze, Kangmar
Lhasa — Shiquanhe	1734	Xigaze, Lhaze, Raka, Coqen, Garze, Gegyai
Shiquanhe — Kashi	1342	Rutog, Hongliutan, Yecheng
Nagqu — Qamdo	764	Sog Xian, Baqen, Dengqen, Riwoqe
Nyingchi — Rawu	345	Tongmai, Bomi
Zetang — Nyingchi	475	Gyaca, Mainling
Shiquanhe — Burang	435	Garyarsa, Moincer, Barga
Lhaze — Burang	935	Saga, Zhongba, Barga

China Tibet Tourism Bureau

China Tibet Tourism Bureau is in charge of the administration of tourism business in Tibet and answering complaints from tourists.

地址:拉萨市园林路
电话:0891-6334330,6334316
传真:0891-6334632
电传:68012 CTTB CN
邮编:850001

ADD:YUANLIN RD, LHASA
TEL:0891-6334330,6334316
FAX:0891-6334632
TLX:68012 CTTB CN
POST CODE:850001

China Tibet Tourism Bureau

How to Get Tour Service and Permit to Enter Tibet

TIBET TOUR MAGAZINE
ADD:YUANLIN RD, LHASA
TEL:0891-6334315,6336042
FAX:0891-6334632
EDITOR:HE ZHONG

Travel agencies and hotels in Tibet can provide all kinds of services for tourists. Group tours are encouraged. A Tibet entrance permit is required. Tour groups can obtain the pass from authorized travel agencies in Tibet. For individuals we have offices in Beijing, Guangzhou, Chengdu, Chongqing, Golmud (Qinghai) to answer your questions and orgainze FIT tours to Tibet. Also in Hongkong and Nepal, we have agencies to organize and receive overseas groups.

BRANCH OFFICE OF THE TIBET TOURISM BUREAU

TIBET TOURISM BUREAU BEIJING OFFICE
ADD: NO. 149 W – GULOU STREET, BEIJING
TEL:010—407 10 96
FAX:010 – 4019831
DIRECTOR:CAO XIAOYU

TIBET TOURISM BUREAU CHENGDU OFFICE
ADD:NO. 10 N – RENMIN RD, CHENGDU
TEL:028 – 3333988
FAX:028 – 3333526
DIRECTOR:WANG XIAOFENG

TIBET TOURISM BUREAU HONGKONG OFFICE
ADD:37/F, TIME TOWER, 393 JAFFA RD, HONGKONG
TEL:0852 – 8383391
FAX:0852 – 8341535
GENERAL MANAGER:DENG KEPING

TIBET TOURISM BUREAU GUANGZHOU OFFICE
ADD: 113 YANJIANG XILU, GUANGZHOU
TEL: 020 – 8866668 – 701
FAX: 020 – 8883519
DIRECTOR: LI ZHIRONG

NAME LIST OF TIBET TRAVEL AGENCIES

TIBET TOURIST CORPORATION
ADD: NO. 208 WEST BEIJING RD, LHASA
TEL: 0891 – 6332980
FAX: 0891 – 6335277
GENERAL MANAGER: TSIWANG SIDA

TIBET CHINA INTERNATIONAL TRAVEL SERVICE
ADD: NO. 208 WEST BEIJING RD, LHASA
TEL: 0891 – 6332980
FAX: 0891 – 6336315
GENERAL MANAGER: TSIWANG SIDA

SHIGATSE CHINA INT'L TRAVEL SERVICE
ADD: ROOM NO. 1120 HOLIDAY INN, LHASA
TEL: 0891 – 6336771-1120
FAX: 0891 – 6332345
GENERAL MANAGER: NGAWANG DIJE

TIBET INT'L SPORTS TRAVEL SERVICE
ADD: NO. 6 E – LINGKOR RD, LHASA
TEL: 0891 – 6322293
FAX: 0891 – 6334855
GENERAL MANAGER: SU PING

LHASA TRAVEL AGENCY
ADD: NO. 27 LINGGYI RD, LHASA
TEL: 0891 – 6332196
FAX: 0891 – 6335765
GENERAL MANAGER: DONG TIANLIN

TSETANG CHINA INT'L TRAVEL SERVICE
ADD: ROOM NO. 1688 HOLIDAY INN, LHASA
TEL: 0891 – 6332221-1688
FAX: 0891 – 6332446
GENERAL MANAGER: ZHANG JINQING

TIBET CHINA YOUTH TRAVEL SERVICE
ADD: NO. 32 E – JINGDREL RD, LHASA
TEL: 0891 – 6332221-1106
FAX: 0891 – 6335588
GENERAL MANAGER: WANG SONGPING

CHINA WORKERS' TRAVEL SERVICE, TIBET BRANCH
ADD: ROOM NO. 1104 HOLIDAY INN, LHASA
TEL: 0891 – 6332221-1104
FAX: 0891 – 6334472
GENERAL MANAGER: G. T. SONAM

TIBET CHINA TRAVEL SERVICE
ADD: NO. 208 W – BEIJING RD, LHASA
TEL: 0891 – 6335046
FAX: 0891 – 6336315
GENERAL MANAGER: TSIWANG SIDA

CHINA GOLDEN BRIDGE TRAVEL, LHASA BRANCH
ADD: NO. 10 MINZU RD, LHASA
TEL: 0891 – 6323828, 6324063
FAX: 0891 – 6335822
GENERAL MANAGER:
ZHANG WANCHENG

NGARI TRAVEL AGENCY
ADD: NO. 4 NORTH SHIQUANHE RD, NGARI
TEL: 08073 – 21799
FAX: 08073 – 21486
GENERAL MANAGER: WANG WEIMING

TIBET SCIENCE TRVEL AGENCY
ADD: NO. 230 W – BEIJING RD, LHASA
TEL: 0891 – 6332217
FAX: 0891 – 6332217
GENERAL MANAGER: KALSANG DOJE

TIBET M.T AND RIVER TRAVEL
ADD: NO. 195 CENTRAL BEIJING RD, LHASA
TEL: 0891 – 6333819, 6333829
FAX: 0891 – 6333828
GENERAL MANAGER:

TIBET ASIA DRAGON TRAVEL AGENCY
ADD: NO. 3 MINZU RD, LHASA
TEL: 0891 – 6332196
FAX: 0891 – 6332196
GENERAL MANAGER: WANG NAIWEN

TIBET TRAFFIC HOLYLAND TRAVEL
ADD: NO. 44 C – BEIJING RD. LHASA
TEL: 0891 – 6324510, 6333931
FAX: 0891 – 6332837
GENERAL MANAGER: TUPDEN

TIBET PLATEAU IRON HORSE TRAVEL
ADD: NO. 1 JIEBAI RD, LHASA
TEL: 0891 – 6323890
FAX: 0891 – 6336793
GENERAL MANAGER: ZHANG XIAOYA

TIBET GANCHEN TRAVEL AGENCY
ADD: NO. 83 E – BEIJING RD, LHASA
TEL: 0891 – 6335365
FAX: 0891 – 6335365
GENERAL MANAGER: MINGMA DUNDROP

TIBET FOREIGN AFFAIRS SERVICE CENTRE
ADD: NO. 18 N – LINGKOR RD, LHASA
TEL: 0891 – 6335051
FAX: 0891 – 6334942
GENERAL MANAGER: MA QINSHENG

NAKCHU TRAVEL AGENCY
ADD: NO. 262 SINE RD, NAKCHU
TEL: 08064 – 22424
FAX: 08064 –
GENERAL MANAGER: ZHANG ZHONGWEI

NYINGCHI TRAVEL AGENCY
ADD: NO. MENTSEKANG RD, LHASA
TEL: 0891 – 6333871, 6336638
FAX: 0891 – 6333563
GENERAL MANAGER: PORPU

TIBET SNOWLAND TRAVEL AGENCY

ADD: ROOM NO. 337 TIBET HOTEL, LHASA
TEL:0891 — 6334966-337
FAX:0891 — 6336648
GENERAL MANAGER:ZHOU SHAOXI

TIBET AIRLINE TRAVEL SERVICE

ADD:NO.14 E — KANGLANG RD, LHASA
TEL:0891 — 6333331
FAX:0891 — 6333330
GENERAL MANAGER:LAKPA WANGDO

TIBET WOMEN'S TRAVEL AGENCY

ADD:NO.13 YUTOK RD, LHASA
TEL:0891 — 6333678
FAX:0891 —
GENERAL MANAGER:DECHEN

TIBET KAILASH TRAVEL AGENCY

ADD:YUANLIN RD, LHASA
TEL:0891 — 6330537
FAX:0891 — 6333598
GENERAL MANAGER:LUOYE

TIBET RELIGIOUS TRAVEL AGENCY

ADD:NO.22 N — LINGKOR RD, LHASA
TEL:0891 — 6336128
FAX:0891 —
GENERAL MANAGER:KALSANG

TIBET FRIENDSHIP TRAVEL AGENCY

ADD:YUANLIN RD, LHASA
TEL:0891 — 6332456
FAX:0891 — 6334533
GENERAL MANAGER:KALSANG

TIBET ARTS TRAVEL SERVICE

ADD:NO.170 C — BEIJING RD, LHASA
TEL:0891 — 6334144
FAX:0891 — 6334143
GENERAL MANAGER: DEQIN LAMU

TIBET SILVER BRIDGE TRAVEL AGENCY

ADD:NO.1 DODE RD, LHASA
TEL:0891 — 6336324
FAX:0891 — 6336896
GENERAL MANAGER:DENZEN NYEMA

TIBET COMFORT TRAVEL SERVICE

ADD:NO.228 W — BEIJING RD, LHASA
TEL:0891 — 6334245
FAX:0891 — 6335052
GENERAL MANAGER:ZAXI

TIBET TRADE TRAVEL AGENCY

ADD:NO.186 C — BEIJING RD, LHASA
TEL:0891 — 6336620
FAX:0891 — 6336322
GENERAL MANAGER:DONG JINGJIANG

LHASA COMPANY CHINA TIBET QOMO-LANGMA TRAVEL WAYS

ADD: ROOM NO. 1112, HOLIDAY INN LHASA
TEL:0891 — 6336863, 6332221-1112
FAX:0891 — 6336861
GENERAL MANAGER:LIN GUITIAN

TIBET POTALA FOLK TRAVEL AGENCY

ADD:NO.49 E — BEIJING RD, LHASA
TEL:0891 — 6324822
FAX:0891 — 6333551
GENERAL MANAGER:DAWA

TIBET NATURAL TRAVEL AGENCY

ADD:ROOM NO.1108 HOLIDAY INN, LHASA
TEL:0891 — 6336655, 6332221-1108
FAX:0891 — 6336855, 6335118
GENERAL MANAGER: WANG HUILING

TIBET INTELLIGENT CULTURAL TOURISM CORP

ADD:NO.2 DOKDE RD, LHASA
TEL:0891 — 6335257
FAX:0891 — 6336538
GENERAL MANAGER:YENONG

TRAVEL AGENCY OF TSETANG HOTEL

ADD:NO.196 C — BEIJING RD, LHASA
TEL:0891 — 6332603, 6326089-246
FAX:0891 — 6332603
GENERAL MANAGER:PUBU TSERING

TIBET TOUR VEHICLE COMPANY

ADD:NO.11 JIEBAI RD, LHASA
TEL:0891 — 6326407
FAX:0891 — 6335227
GENERAL MANAGER:DOPGYEL

LHOKA SPORTS TRAVEL AGENCY

ADD:
TEL:0893 —
FAX:0893 —
GENERAL MANAGER:WANGDUR

SHIGATSE TOUR VEHICLE COMPANY

ADD: NO. 15 C — JINGDREL RD, SHI-GATSE
TEL:0892 — 23502
FAX:0892 —
GENERAL MANAGER:DOPLA

TIBET TOUR SERVICE COMPANY

ADD:NO.39 YULTOK RD, LHASA
TEL:0891 — 6322029
FAX:0891 —
GENERAL MANAGER:LI ZHONGYUN

TIBET TRAVELS AND TOURS

ADD:NO.1 MINGZU RD, LHASA
TEL:0891 — 6324305, 6332221-71305
FAX:0891 — 6334957
GENERAL MANAGER:YULGYEL

LHASA TOUR VEHICLE COMPANY

ADD:NO.31, NARCHEN RD, LHASA
TEL:0891 — 6323762
FAX:0891 — 6323762
GENERAL MANAGER:SONAM TARGYE

SHIGATSE TOUR VEHICLE SERVICE

ADD: NO. 15 C — JINGDREL RD, SHI-GATSE
TEL:0892 —
FAX:0892 —
GENERAL MANAGER:

CHINA TIBET QOMOLANGMA TRAVEL WAYS LTD

ADD: 37/F, TIME TOWER, 393 JAFFE, ROAD, HONGKONG
TEL:0852 — 8383391
FAX:0852 — 8341535
GENERAL MANAGER:DENG KEPING

TIBET TOURISM BUREAU KATHMANDU OFFICE

ADD:NO.01147 POST BOX,KATHMANDU, NEPAL
TEL:00977 — 1 — 410411
FAX:00977 — 1 — 227538, 419778
DIRECTOR:TSEDOJE

NAME LIST OF TIBET TOUR HOTELS

HOLIDAY INN LHASA
ADD:NO.1 MINGZU RD, LHASA
TEL:0891 – 6332221
FAX:0891 – 6335796
GENERAL MANAGER:JEGME

TIBET HOTEL LHASA
ADD:NO.221 WEST BEIJING RD, LHASA
TEL:0891 – 6334966
FAX:0891 – 6336787
GENERAL MANAGER:CHAMBA DANTAR

SUNLIGHT HOTEL
ADD:NO.27 LINGGYI RD, LHASA
TEL:0891 – 6322227
FAX:0891 –6335675
GENERAL MANAGER:DONG TIANLIN

HIMALAYA HOTEL
ADD:NO.6 LINGKOR RD, LHASA
TEL:0891 – 6334082
FAX:0891 – 6334855
GENERAL MANAGER:SUPING

SHIGATSE HOTEL
ADD:NO.13 JIEFANG RD, SHIGATSE
TEL:0892 – 22525, 22526
FAX:0892 –
GENERAL MANAGER:WANGLA

TSETANG HOTEL
ADD: NO. 21 NEDONG RD, TSETANG, LHOKA
TEL:0893 – 21809
FAX:0893 – 21640
GENERAL MANAGER:SUNAM DANTSEN

GYANGSTE HOTEL
ADD:GYANGTSE
TEL:08019 –
FAX:08019 –
GENERAL MANAGER:LUNDROP
                    TSERING

SHIQUANHE HOTEL
ADD: NO. 3 NORTH SHIQUANHE RD, NGARI
TEL:08073 – 21799
FAX:08073 – 21486
GENERAL MANAGER:WANG WEIMING

NAKCHU HOTEL
ADD:NO.262 EAST SINI RD, NAKCHU
TEL:08064 – 22424
FAX:08064 –
GENERAL MANAGER: ZHANG ZHONG WEI

PLATEAU HOTEL
ADD:NO.74 NACHEN RD, LHASA
TEL:0891 – 6324916
FAX:0891 – 6326084
GENERAL MANAGER:LUBDEN

BANAKXUL HOTEL
ADD:NO.43 EAST BEIJING RD, LHASA
TEL:0891 – 6323829
FAX:0891 –
GENERAL MANAGER:LUBSANG

GYIRE HOTEL
ADD:NO.105 EAST BEIJING RD, LHASA
TEL:0891 – 6323462
FAX:0891 – 6323987
GENERAL MANAGER:TSIRING DIJE

KADA HOTEL
ADD:NO.36 EAST JINGDRUL RD, LHASA
TEL:0891 – 6323430, 6325865
FAX:0891 –
GENERAL MANAGER:BANBA

YAK HOTEL
ADD:NO.100 EAST BEIJING RD, LHASA
TEL:0891 – 6323496
FAX:0891 –
GENERAL MANAGER:KUNCHOK

SNOWLAND HOTEL
ADD:NO.4 MENTSIKANG RD, LHASA
TEL:0891 – 6323687
FAX:0891 –
GENERAL MANAGER:GYALO

WELCOME HOTEL
ADD:NO.34 ULTOK RD, LHASA
TEL:0891 – 6322184
FAX:0891 –
GENERAL MANAGER: TSERING YANG-ZONG

THE RESTAURANT OF THE GOVERN-MENT OF TIBET AUTONOMOUS REGION
ADD: NO. 196 CENTRAL BEIJING RD, LHASA
TEL:0891 – 6326091
FAX:0891 –
GENERAL MANAGER:CHEN BAOYUE

FRIENDSHIP HOTEL
ADD:YUANLIN RD, LHASA
TEL:0891 – 6332456
FAX:0891 – 6334533
GENERAL MANAGER:KALSANG

TINGRI EVEREST HOTEL
ADD:BELBA, TINGRI
TEL:08026 –
FAX:08026 –
GENERAL MANAGER:

PURANG HOTEL
ADD:NO.4 KUNGA RD, PURANG NGARI
TEL:08074 –
FAX:08074 –
GENERAL MANAGER:KALSANG

SAMDROTSE HOTEL
ADD: NO. 2 GUNCHOKLING RD, SHI-
GATSE
TEL: 0892 – 22252, 22280
FAX: 0892 –
GENERAL MANAGER: CHAMCHOK

ZHANGMU HOTEL
ADD: ZHANGMU
TEL: 08074 – 26305
FAX: 08074 –
GENERAL MANAGER: SONAMCHAKPA

KAILASH HOTEL
ADD: TARCHEN, PURANG, NGARI
TEL: 08074 –
FAX: 08074 –
GENERAL MANAGER: TSEDRAK

NYINGCHI RESTAURANT
ADD: BAYI
TEL: 0894 –
FAX: 0894 –
GENERAL MANAGER: SONAM

DANTSEN HOTEL
ADD: SHIGATSE
TEL: 0892 – 22018
FAX: 0892 –
GENERAL MANAGER: DANTSEN

BEIJING QOMOLANGMA HOTEL
ADD: NO. 149 WEST GULOU STREET,
BEIJING
TEL: 010 – 4018822
FAX: 010 – 4019831
GENERAL MANAGER:

TIBET HOTEL
ADD: NO. 10 NORTH RENMIN RD,
CHENGDU
TEL: 028 – 3333988
FAX: 028 – 3333526
GENERAL MANAGER: HE SHENGQIU

XIAN QOMOLANGMA HOTEL
ADD: NO. 55 EAST YOUYI RD, XI'AN
TEL: 029 – 5261980
FAX: 029 – 5261017
GENERAL MANAGER: ZHANG BOYI

TIBET TOURIST DEVELOPMENT CORPORATION
ADD: YUANLIN RD, LHASA
TEL: 0891-6332456
FAX: 0891-6334533
GENERAL MANAGER: KALSANG

TIBET TOURISM DEVELOPMENT CORPO RATION, CHENGDU BRANCH

ADD: NO. 6 SOUTHERN BUILDING, 61/ SOUTHERN TAISHENG RD,
CHENGDU, CHINA
TEL: 028 – 6627931 – 618, 613
FAX: 028 – 6752998   POST CODE: 610017

Welcome to Tibet to tour on the roof of the world.
Have a pleasant journey and good luck!

Ancient statue of Buddha (made in Yuan Dynasty) blessing tourists a good journey

TRAVEL ON THE ROOF OF THE WORLD
——CHINA TIBET TOUR

中国旅游出版社出版
(北京建国门内大街甲九号)
中国旅游出版社发行
(电话:513.8866－2024)
深圳彩视电分有限公司制版
东莞威骏彩印钉装有限公司印刷

开本:889×1194
印张:15.5
1995 年 2 月　第一版第一次印刷
印数:2000(英文)
ISBN 7－5032－1138－5/K·171
013800